The Philosopher's Enigma

From the Lives of Things

The perfect skin of things is stretched across them
as snugly as a circus tent.
Evening nears.
Welcome, darkness.
Farewell, daylight.
We're like eyelids, assert things,
we touch eyes, hair, darkness,
light, India, Europe.

Suddenly I find myself asking: "Things,
do you know suffering?
Were you ever hungry, down and out?
Have you cried? Do you know fear,
shame? Have you learned jealousy, envy,
small sins, not of commission,
but not cured by absolution either?
Have you loved, and died,
at night, wind opening the windows, absorbing
the cool heart? Have you tasted
age, time, bereavement?"
Silence.
On the wall, the needle of a barameter dances.

—Adam Zagajewski, Canvas—Poems

The days of our age are three score and ten
And though men be so strong,
That they come to fourscore years,
Yet is their strength then but labor and sorrow,
So soon it passeth away and we are gone.

—The Book of Common Prayer

The state of the universe and its contents, like
ourselves, are completely determined by the laws
of physics, up to the limit set by the uncertainty
principle. So much for free will.

—Stephen W. Hawking, *The Theory of Everything:*
The Origin and Fate of the Universe

There is hope of a tree, if it be cut down, that it
will sprout again, and that the tender branch thereof
will not cease. . . . But man dieth, and wasteth away,
yea: man giveth up the ghost, and where is he?

—Book of Job 14:7-10

The Philosopher's Enigma
God, Body and Soul

God, Disembodied Spirits, Free Will, Determinism,
and the Mind-Body Problem

Richard A. Watson

Emeritus Professor of Philosophy , Washington University in
St. Louis; Affiliate Professor of Philosophy, University of Montana

ST. AUGUSTINE'S PRESS
South Bend, Indiana

Manufactured in the United States of America

1 2 3 4 5 6 19 18 17 16 15 14 13

Library of Congress Cataloging in Publication Data
Watson, Richard A., 1931–
The philosopher's enigma: God, body and soul:
God, disembodied spirits, free will, determinism,
and the mind-body problem / Richard A. Watson.
p. cm.
Includes bibliographical references and index.
ISBN 978-1-58731-649-4 (alk. paper)
1. Christianity – Controversial literature. I. Title.
BL2775.3.W38 2013
212 – dc23   2012039818

∞ The paper used in this publication meets the minimum requirements of the American National Standard for Information Sciences Permanence of Paper for Printed Materials, ANSI Z39.481984.

ST. AUGUSTINE'S PRESS
www.staugustine.net

Acknowledgments

I thank Eldon Dryer, Sharon Dreyer, Patrick Henry, Justin Leiber, Janet Levy, William Lycan, Jose Raimundo Maia-Neto, Steven Nadler, Richard Popkin, Paul Steward, Douglas Walker, Anna Watson, and Patty Jo Watson for corrections, comments, and discussions. I am especially indebted to Henry Shapiro for his corrections, suggestions, and meticulous editing.

CONTENTS

Prelude

This book is written to be of interest to and accessible to both professional philosophers and general readers.

The issues and problems considered herein are older than the Old Testament, and probably some of them were discussed around campfires 40,000 years ago.

Does God exist?

Does the notion of an all-powerful God make sense?

In what does belief in God consist?

Will my soul survive the death of my body?

Can angels help and ghosts harm me?

Do I have free will?

Is my mind my brain?

Chapter 1.

God

When my daughter Anna was six and seven years old, I read great swatches of the Bible to her out loud, from both the Old and New Testaments, starting with Genesis and ending with Revelation. It was far from easy going. She had learned to read when she was four, and at one point she followed along and did not allow me to skip a single "begat." The most difficult times were when she would react with disgust or outrage, and I had to bribe her to continue. For example, the story of Job was totally contrary to her apparently innate sense of justice. When we finally did get through it, she asked, "Were the sons and daughters returned to Job the *same* sons and daughters that were killed?" I had to admit that they were not. She gave me a look of utter scorn, slid off my lap, and it took me several days to convince her to continue.

The greatest problem was in the beginning, in the Garden of Eden. She was mesmerized by the story of the Fall, but not enough to dull her child's steel-trap mind. When it was over, Adam and Eve banished, their progeny cursed, and all of humankind doomed, she kept objecting, "But God *made* Adam! God *made* Adam sin! How could God punish Adam and Eve when he made them and made them do what they did? God made the serpent, and he tricked Eve, and he made Adam eat the apple! It's not fair! God made Adam do it!"

I admitted that this was a problem.

Later Anna had similar difficulties with Jesus. At the age of seven, she was not yet up to challenging virgin birth or Jesus as the Son of God, but Jesus on the cross was a real burden to her. Particularly when Jesus says, "My God, my God, why hast Thou forsaken me?" Yes, why? And here the problem of God's creating the world and everything in it arose again. Anna had heard and read enough books to know that the plot was rotten. Even Christ's rising from the dead did not fix it. What kind of charade is this (not her words, but her perception), with God setting up Adam to sin, making all Adam's progeny suffer from it, and then sending down his Only Begotten Son to die on the cross to pay for all those sins? Nope. It doesn't wash.

We did get through the Bible, more or less, and Anna remembers it if not exactly fondly, at least as a landmark in her being-read-to childhood. At the end—Revelation—she doted on the curses, the seven plagues, the dragon with seven heads and ten horns and seven crowns upon the seven heads. Throughout she liked the locusts, as she was particularly fond of insects. What a climax, with all the sinners being swallowed up into Hell! By then she thought she understood, and trembled at horrors in fascinated delight, particularly in response to the Book of Revelation. But this also meant that she got into a fistfight at camp with a little Catholic girl over the claim (Anna's) that God was just made up, like Santa Claus.

My wife Pat and I were raised in northern Iowa as Methodists, and we went to Sunday School, Church, and Youth Fellowship until we were eighteen and left for college. Church in a small town of twelve hundred souls was almost entirely social. We did take communion on Easter. I cannot remember ever having taken any of it seriously, nor have I ever had a religious feeling or experience in my life. Pat says she thinks she believed until she was about fourteen, and then it all just drifted away. As adults, we have never gone to church, nor did our daughter, except when we visited our parents, who as far as we could make out were never very religious, although they participated fully in all functions of the Methodist Church. Anna's Swedish grandmother, who was Lutheran and after whom Anna was named, was horrified that Anna was not baptized, but none of her schemes for accomplishing this got anywhere. So we raised a little heathen.

If my religious sensibilities are at most agnostic, why then did I read the Bible to my daughter? That's easy. We live in a largely Christian country with intellectual and cultural foundations in Christian Western Civilization, and the King James Bible is the most important and magnificent book in that tradition. I read it to my daughter not just for the finest writing style in English, but also for all the moral precepts and cautionary tales that saturate our culture.

Our way of life is predominantly Christian. No child of mine was going to be deprived of this heritage simply because her parents were not true believers. She absorbed the Bible the way she absorbed *Robinson Crusoe, Gulliver's Travels, The Canterbury Tales, The Way of All Flesh*, the main plays of Shakespeare, and numerous other classics of Western literature. Not to forget the *Momintroll* books by Tove Jansen. I never read anything to her that I did not want to read for my own pleasure. I recommend this course to young parents who might otherwise get trapped into reading over and over again the same books about bunnies, although *Goodnight Moon* is OK.

In one sense it does not matter what you read to your children. Partly they just want your attention, to hear your voice, anyway. But if you are going to read to them, you might as well read good stuff, and moreover, they understand a lot more than you might think.

Then the day came when Anna went away to college. She majored in Japanese, then lived three years in Tokyo, came back for an MFA in Creative Writing, and landed one year in Boston where she signed up for an MA in Race Relations in a program run by the five Boston area seminaries. But, alas, there were not enough students for that program, so they told her that if she would sign up for an MA in Feminist Liberation Theology, and take two courses in Theology, she could also take the required Race Relations courses she wanted. It would just be that her MA would be in Feminist Liberation Theology. OK, she said. (I have always been suspicious of this. If she could take all the courses for Race Relations, why couldn't she get an MA in it? I think they just wanted to graduate a class in Feminist Liberation Theology.)

About six weeks into the program, Anna called home. Pat answered the phone. "Why didn't you tell me," Anna said to her mother, "that religion was so important?"

"You knew religion was important," Pat said.

"Yes, well, I suppose," Anna said. "But I didn't know they *believed* it."

Her two theology courses were taught by theologians who gave expositions of major critiques of Christianity. Anna liked the courses, but she said they were extremely hard on some of the students who had never before had to face opposition to their beliefs. She

3

finished her courses, wrote her thesis, and graduated in one year. It was in fact a two-year program, the second year to be taken up with writing a thesis, but Anna wrote hers in six weeks. Pat and I went to the graduation.

Anna's thesis professor told us what a fine student Anna was to get her MA in only one year. As he walked away, she whispered, "I just wanted to get the Hell out of there."

It was not, she explained later, that she did not like the courses, some of which were among the best she had ever had. It was that she found the true believers among her classmates spooky.

I have set out to write this book because since I was ten or eleven, I have wondered why anyone would believe in God, and if one did believe in God, why the Christian God? Fifty of those years have been spent studying and teaching philosophy, which only made me more puzzled. Western philosophy is shot through with the Christian God. I used to joke that I was going to write a book with the title *Western Philosophy without God*. It would be three and one-half pages long. In his *God in Modern Philosophy*, James Collins covers less than a fourth of Western Philosophy, and the book contains 476 pages of small print. During all these years I have been baffled by the in-my-face fact that thousands of thinkers who were as bright as I am (and many much brighter) believed in God. I know a number of people, including some of my relatives, with incredibly sharp minds who believe in God. How throughout the ages could people with such immense powers of reason believe in God?

I decided that it was time for me to undertake a serious investigation into the problem of why anyone would believe in God, and because it is after all my heritage, of why anyone would be a Christian. Because the heart of this book is not where I arrive but how I get there, I will say immediately that what serious study of the literature has shown me (what any believer would have told me) is that faith, not reason, is the foundational support of belief in God. Everyone knows more or less what reason is, but what, precisely, is faith? Faith appears to be the opposite of reason.

Faith definitely does not depend on reason even though supplementary to faith there are a number of rational arguments for the existence of God—which break down into three main ones: the cosmological (God as first cause or Creator); the ontological (existence as a necessary property of God, for if God did not exist, He would not be God); and the argument from design (the world is so complex that there had to be a Designer). But as Saint Thomas Aquinas points out, these are not conclusive proofs; rather, they are presented simply to bolster the faith of believers. But if reason does not lead to a proof that God exists, why do people believe?

There are obvious and perfectly good reasons why some people believe in God and Christianity. The vast majority of people—I generalize from some forty years of teaching philosophy—do not see or understand the problems such belief raises. I would not exactly say that these believers are not very bright. They may just have minds that do not focus on problems of meaning, inconsistency, contradiction, weakness of inference, and lack of evidence. Perhaps some of them believe just because it makes life easier for them, and dismiss any further thought on the matter. Blaise Pascal suspected that René Descartes believed simply as a matter of convenience, to stay out of trouble with the Catholic Church, and to divest his mind of religious concerns so he could concentrate on his scientific work. This is possibly true of Descartes, but I think he probably just didn't worry about it. (See my biography of Descartes: *Cogito Ergo Sum: The Life of René Descartes.*)

Others believe in God and Christianity for aesthetic reasons— they find the ritual and ceremony beautiful. Then there are psychological reasons. Belief gives some people confidence for living. For example, if the members of the Notre Dame football team pray before each game, perhaps it helps them play better.

Some believe out of perversity, as did Tertullian and Søren Kierkegaard who said they believe in Christianity because it is absurd. There are also those who believe because of the comfort the companionship, the living, or the power that being a part of the Church gives them.

And some believe because they are afraid of dying. They would like their consciousness, their thoughts, their minds—their souls—to survive the death of their bodies.

Finally, the vast majority of Christians believe because somehow they just *know* that God exists and that Christianity is the True religion. These last, particularly those very intelligent true believers who persist in their belief in the face of all logical problems (e.g., if God created Himself, He must have existed before he existed) and horrible events (e.g., if God created the world, then He countenanced the Holocaust), really puzzle me.

Most Christians believe in God just on faith and do not try to reason about doctrines, or even to understand them. After all, Jesus says, "Be ye as little children" (*Matthew* 18.3). So you are asked to believe that Jesus is your Savior without concerning yourself for a moment about what this actually involves when spelled out in detail. Just trust your priest or preacher.

Large numbers of people have grown up in societies in which they were taught to believe in some supernatural religion, and never thought to question it. The Jesuits say, give them a boy until he is seven years old, and he will be a Catholic all his life—even if he professes not to be a believer.

On the other hand, some people think belief is automatic, natural, inborn. Maybe belief in God is just a part of human nature. This does not mean that it would be genetically hardwired, because it does not develop in everyone. Jesse M. Bering suggests that

> The ability to attribute consciousness to invisible, supernatural agents may have come about as a by-product of people's ability to reason about other human minds . . . [then if] individuals thought that they were constantly being watched by invisible beings . . . human beings might believe that omnipotent deities would punish them if they did wrong . . . [so] belief in such omnipotent forces could have then increased genetic fitness by preventing cheating behaviors that could result in social repercussions. (pp. 143, 145–146)

Pascal Boyer has studied human prehistory back several hundred thousand years, and he also postulates that belief that there are invisible and powerful beings who know everything and are watching what we do might make our dealings with one another more honest and cooperative. At the same time, one might soon get the idea that one could exert some control over such supernatural beings by begging from or bribing them. If you can get such superior beings to tell you things or do things for you, this obviously puts you at an advantage over other people who do not have such help.

Again, this does not require that belief in the supernatural be genetically determined. It could arise out of behavior and experience, for example, on the model of your father who seemed to be all-powerful and all-knowing when you were a child. It would be nice to have that sense of security even when you were grown up.

There is no question but that religion and belief in the supernatural can have many beneficial results. But one contemporary question—in the modern world of weapons of mass destruction—is whether or not dogmatic religious belief that you have the Truth and that your God is *the* God is advantageous to the human race.

Consider, for example, this scenario. The pious rulers of a Christian nation are in conflict with the pious rulers of a Muslim nation. Each has enough nuclear weapons to wipe out the other, which in the process would destroy most animal life on the planet above the size of cockroaches. Surely no madness would drive these leaders to unleash the bombs. But consider: Christians believe that at the end of time, the earth will be destroyed in a massive battle, and all true believers will be transported bodily to Heaven. Muslims also believe in a similar end-of-days Armageddon.

Mutually assured destruction, in that light, looks like a win-win, no-lose situation.

That could never happen? In an age of science and reason you might think not. But the forces of religious orthodoxy have more power today than they have had since the late Middle Ages. Armageddon and Jihad, God and Allah, may rule the day.

You can watch television and read the newspapers to follow that story. In this first chapter of this book, I am concerned neither with the evolution of human religious belief, nor with possible apocalyptic outcomes of that belief, but with the question of why anyone today would believe in the existence of God.

There is something in the human makeup that leads many people to accept logical contradictions (e.g., the doctrine of the Trinity that God is both One and Three) and miracles that go against nature (e.g., Jesus rising from the dead). Tales full of logical and natural impossibilities (there are many in the Bible) obviously have horrified and delighted, distressed and comforted, guided and misguided, and above all convinced human beings of their truth since the origin of our species. You know who is the greatest contemporary creator of such supernatural stories: Stephen King. Perhaps it is just as well that he did not come into his maturity with the aspiration of creating a new religion.

I used to tell my students that the world is divided into two kinds of people: those who want to know things and those who want to own things. This book is about two other kinds of people: those who take faith and mystery as sufficient ground for the existence of God, and those who take reason and experience as the necessary basis of all knowledge. Those who base religious knowledge on faith can still base scientific knowledge on reason and experience. But those who take reason and experience as a necessary basis of all knowledge cannot profess any knowledge that is based solely on faith. Thus the division between these two kinds of people can be characterized as follows: Those who profess to have some knowledge based on faith alone can believe in the supernatural; those who believe that all knowledge must be based on reason and experience alone cannot believe in the supernatural. Supernaturalists do use reason and experience in ordinary life, but believe that religious knowledge can be illogical, contradictory, and irrational, or more gently, incomprehensible to the human intellect. The naturalists believe that all knowledge must be logical, consistent, and rational. For them, there are no unfathomable mysteries, nothing supernatural; there is only rational knowledge and ignorance.

The most rigorous foundational source of Christian doctrine is the third-century theologian Saint Augustine. He did not come to his faith in easy steps. All Christians should read his *Confessions*. Saint Augustine believes on faith, but he works out Christian doctrine on strictly logical grounds. This makes believers who depend solely on faith impatient, but thinking about God is not easy. Saint Augustine's expositions of Christian doctrines, particularly about God, are as clear and as astute as any we have. I take them to be foundational to Christianity.

Like virtually all major religions, Christianity begins with God. But in the beginning, there was nothing. Out of this nothing, God created the world as we know it. James Ussher, who was Archbishop of Armagh in Ireland, figured out from Bible chronology that God created the Heavens and the earth out of nothing at 9:00 in the morning on October 23, 4004 B.C. Or, if you want, you can accept the calculations of the contemporary physicist Stephen Hawking that the universe began with a Big Bang nearly fourteen billion years ago. Some scientists believe that God caused the Big Bang. In some readings, this is equivalent to creating the universe out of nothing. But what about God's existence? God exists neither in time nor in space. He is neither temporal nor spatial. God has spiritual existence in eternity. For Him, there is no sequence of time as we experience it. So from God's viewpoint, our world did not begin: it always was, or, from God's viewpoint, it always *is*.

But what about God Himself? God is *causa sui*, that is, He creates Himself. That means that He has to exist before He exists, that He has to be there to create Himself before He is there. This is a circular fallacy in logic, the claim that A precedes B, but also B precedes A. But if God is eternal and thus exists neither in space nor time, then there is no before and after. So temporal order is ruled out. You might say that this means A and B exist at the same time, but that is wrong. They do not exist in time, they just exist. But what about causal order? If A is required to cause B, and B is required to cause A, both of these requirements would be satisfied in a non-spatial, non-temporal, eternal realm where there is no before and after. In effect, A and B would be co-eternal, so presumably A could be the cause of B, and B could be the cause of A "at the same time." On the other hand, because there is no beginning in an eternal realm, to say that God caused Himself is no more than to say that God exists. This reduces to saying that God exists because He exists, which is just another circular argument. Why does God exist? Because He exists. I am that I am. (Exodus 3:14)

Here is as good a place as any to introduce the fundamental mystery of God (and of Christianity) that appeals to so many people. In religious contexts, mystery always implies incomprehensibility, often in the sense that the description of what is mysterious is a logical contradiction. To say that God creates Himself and the world out of nothing is incomprehensible in this sense. It is to say that something comes from nothing. But how could that be? It is a mystery. Human beings love mysteries. In the 1940s, one of my favorite radio programs was "I Love a Mystery."

But the mystery of God raises a problem for Christian theologians. If God created the temporal, material world out of His own eternal, immaterial Being, this would appear to make the world Divine. If the world comes out of God, and God is Divine, then the world must be Divine. But this is pantheism—the view that everything is God—and for Christians pantheism is a heresy. Spinoza was excommunicated by the Jews for saying that God and the world are one. But back up a moment. It may be logical to say that what is created by the Divine must itself be Divine, but God is not bound by logic. God can very well create a world that is not Divine, i.e., not itself God.

The pantheistic view that everything is God is a heresy. For Christians, God and the world are utterly different from one another. So utterly different, in fact, that it is a mystery how they can have anything to do with one another. God is perfect, but the world is imperfect; God is eternal, but the world is in time; God is an immaterial spirit and the world consists of matter; God is wholly good, but there is evil in the world.

But God did create the world, and He acts in the world by causing miracles. *How* God can create the world and act in it is an utter mystery, that is, it is totally unintelligible. Don't worry about it. God can do anything.

The ancient philosopher Plotinus suggested that perhaps the world is an emanation from God, and the farther the emanation gets from God, the less perfect it is. So what was perfect, eternal, and all good in God gets attenuated into our imperfect, temporal, and partly evil world. But this emanation theory is silly. Of course the notion of distance out from the source God is just a metaphor, but even so, God is God, and whatever way He projects Himself, the projection would not lose the eternally perfect non-temporality and non-spatiality that characterize God. Further, Plotinus says that although God is wholly good, evil increases in strength the farther away the emanation is from God. But again, this would be to make something (evil) come from nothing (lack of evil in God). Or it would make evil come from its opposite, from good in God. And again, the "distance" an emanation is from God would make no difference whatsoever to the characteristics of God. If God is non-temporal, non-spatial, and all good, then so would be God's emanations. No matter how far away they might be from God, the emanations would not lose the full strength or nature of God's perfections. So the metaphor of God's characteristics attenuating the farther they are projected from their source in God makes no sense at all, whether meant literally (in which case it is false) or metaphorically (in which case the metaphor is not applicable to God).

The problem with all that reasoning, some believers will say, is that I am taking everything so *literally*. You cannot take talk of God literally, because if you do, you generate contradictions, which are literally and logically meaningless. My reply is that I just follow commonsense logic. But to understand God-talk, true believers say, one needs inspiration, one needs faith, one needs uncommon sense.

So let's back up. God created Himself and the world. Out of God's non-temporality, non-spatiality, goodness, and perfect being, He created our temporal, spatial, partly evil, and imperfect world. Reasoning is all well and good, but God is beyond reason, and can do this seemingly impossible thing because God is all-powerful and can do anything at all. But this conclusion itself depends on reasoning that God can do anything because God is all-powerful. So believers use reason when it goes their way, and they dismiss reason when they want to reject its results.

I am baffled. Yes, I know, I lack something the believer has. I lack true belief. I lack faith. I cannot imagine what the believer has going for himself. Look, I could revert to the twelve-year-old Sunday School smarty-pants I was in my youth who tried to get Miss MacAnnany's goat by asking her if God is so all-powerful, then can He do what He cannot do? Can God create a stone too heavy for God to lift? Miss MacAnnany should have answered: Of course! Because God can do anything. God can lift a stone that is too heavy for Him to lift! Instead, she just gave me a baleful eye, and went on with the lesson.

If you are a True Believer, if you have faith, perhaps you see or feel the sense of mystery that is involved here. True religious mysteries involve the assertion of logical contradictions. Literally, these contradictory statements have no meaning. If you say that something is both green and not green, you are literally not saying that that thing has any property at all. Can God do or create things and situations whose descriptions are literal contradictions? If you think so, hang on. You have some heavy guns supporting you.

One defender of mystery is the seventeenth-century mathematician and philosopher, René Descartes, known as the father of modern philosophy and science. Descartes considered whether or not God could make a contradiction such as 2 + 3 = 4 be true, so that 2 and 3 things actually add up to 4 things. He said that of course God can make such contradictions true. God can create such things as square circles, but we cannot understand how, or what a square circle is. It is a mystery. So quit fussing about it. This is the response of a true believer.

Problems about contradictions do not bother many Christian believers today. But there was a virtual war fought over the Trinity in England in the eighteenth century, between Trinitarians who believe that God is the Father, the Son, and the Holy Ghost (1 = 3, you see) and Unitarians who want to exorcise the contradictions from Christian doctrine. The Father, the Son, and the Holy Ghost are the same thing (1 = 1). In 1696, a major Anti-Trinitarian, John Toland, published a book with the title *Christianity Not Mysterious*, in which he fastens on just the sense of the word "mysterious" that I am discussing here. He points out that the Catholic solution of saying that the meanings of contradictory statements in the Bible are to be found in the writings of the Church Fathers is useless, because the Church Fathers themselves contradict one another. More to the point, the Church Fathers contribute to making Christianity mysterious by defending contradictory Christian doctrines. Toland wanted to rid Christianity of incomprehensible doctrines that literally are meaningless contradictions.

Toland set himself a hopeless task. Here is the full title of his treatise:

> CHRISTIANITY NOT MYSTERIOUS: or, A Treatise Shewing, That there is nothing in the GOSPEL Contrary to REASON, Nor ABOVE it: And that no Christian Doctrine can be properly Call'd a MYSTERY

He carries on bravely:

> The *Divines* . . . gravely tell us *we must adore what we
> cannot comprehend.* . . . The worst on-t is, they are not all of
> a Mind. . . . Some of 'em say the *Mysteries of the Gospel* are
> to be understood only in the Sense of the *Antient Fathers.* But
> that is so multifarious, and inconsistent with itself, as to make
> it impossible for any Body to believe so many Contradictions
> at once . . . [Councils and the Pope are no better than anyone
> else because they were not appointed by Christ.] . . . Some
> will have us always believe *what the literal sense [of
> Scripture] imports,* with little or no sense for *Reason,* which
> they reject as not fit to be employ'd about the reveal'd Part of
> Religion. Others assert, that we may use *Reason,* as the
> Instrument, but not the rule of our Belief. The first contend,
> some *Mysteries* may be, or at least seem to be *Contrary to
> Reason,* and yet be receiv'd by Faith. The second, that no
> *Mystery* is contrary to *Reason,* but that all are *above it.* Both
> of 'em from different Principles agree, that several Doctrines
> of the *New Testament* belong no farther to the Enquiries of
> *Reason,* than to prove 'em divinely reveal'd, and that they are
> properly *Mysteries* still. On the contrary, we hold that *Reason*
> is the only foundation of all Certitude; and that nothing
> reveal'd, whether as to its *Manner* or Existence, is more
> exempted from its Disquisitions, than the ordinary
> Phenomena of Nature. (pp. 1–7)

The contradictions of the Trinitarians proliferate, and Toland sets
out to straighten all of them out in logical terms. But his is a hopeless
endeavor because the believers do not care that Christian doctrine is
contradictory, nor do they want it to be explained.

Toland argues (as do the Logical Positivists of the 1930s and after)
that logical contradictions are meaningless, so they cannot refer to
anything, and therefore they should not be part of Christian doctrine:

> To say, for instance, that *a Ball is white and black at once*
> [all over], is to say just nothing. (p. 27). . . . *Four* may be cal-
> l'd *Five* in Heaven; but the Name only is chang'd, the Thing
> remains the same (p. 29).

In particular, Toland speaks of such *"Absurdities* [as] *Transubstantiation."* (p. 25) So, "When we say . . . *that nothing is impossible with God,* we mean whatever is [logically] possible in it self." (p. 40) He says that *"Contradiction* is only another word for Impossible." (p. 150) Finally he burns all his bridges to Christianity by saying that

> No *Miracle* . . . is contrary to Reason. . . . Therefore, all those *Miracles* are fictitious, wherein there occur any Contradictions, as that *Christ* was born without opening any Passage out of the *Virgin's* Body. (p. 151–152)

In that same year, 1696, Edward Stillingfleet published

> *A Discourse in Vindication of the Doctrine of the Trinity, With an Answer to the Late Socinian Objections against it from Scripture, Antiquity, and Reason*

Toland held views like those of the seventeenth-century philosopher John Locke, for whom no proposition that states a contradiction can be meaningful. Stillingfleet defended Christian doctrines that are literal contradictions by saying that the Bible is God's word, and that miracles are the foundation of Christianity. In other words mystery, in the form of contradiction, is at the foundation of Christianity.

Stillingfleet's views have presided, and it is not surprising that Toland is viewed as one of the founders of Unitarianism, that has evolved into the view that God is not a person, and so strictly speaking is not Christian at all. Christians believe in a personal God.

In Christian doctrine, there are three major logical contradictions. The primary contradiction is that God is in three persons: the Father, the Son, and the Holy Ghost. 1 = 3.

The second major mystery in the sense of being a logical contradiction is the doctrine that Jesus is both Divine and human, both God and man, at the same time. But God is perfect, eternal, and all good, whereas man is imperfect, exists in time, and is a sinner. It is a logical contradiction, then, to say that Jesus is both Divine and human. It is a mystery.

The third mysterious doctrine, one that led John Calvin to break with the Catholic Church, has to do with the Eucharist. There are

14

many problems here. How can bread and wine be replaced with Christ's flesh and blood, but still look and taste like bread and wine? Besides that, how can Christ's limited amount of flesh and blood be distributed over virtually unlimited pieces of bread and cups of wine? The logical contradiction here is that 1 = many.

For most Christians, and for most believers of most religions, a major and strong appeal of their religion is the existence of such mysteries, of doctrines that are literally logical contradictions. This attraction to logical contradictions just seems to be a fact about the human intellect. Even when people recognize that logical contradictions are impossible, even that they are meaningless, they are drawn to belief in them. But belief in what? The words are there but contradictions have no sense, because contradictions literally mean nothing at all. When one says "God is the Father, the Son, and the Holy Ghost," one is saying nothing at all. Or so say logicians and those who hold that only logically consistent statements have any meaning. On this view, when someone asserts belief in a statement that is a contradiction, he is asserting belief in nothing at all.

But this has not deterred believers throughout the ages. For example, in the third century A.D., Tertullian said, "I believe because it is absurd." By "absurd," he means contradictory. He said that when one could truly believe that snow is black, then one could be a Christian. In the nineteenth century, Søren Kierkegaard said that he believed that Christ was his Savior because the most absurd thing he could think of was the existence of a being, Jesus, Who was both man and God at the same time, Who could take the blame for sins that Kierkegaard had committed. One possibility is that Tertullian and Kierkegaard were just being perverse, but I believe that they truly meant what they said.

Tertullian and Kierkegaard are stressing the point that human beings have no knowledge of God at all. The infinite nature of God rules out God's being comprehensible by finite human understanding. So God is ineffable, hidden, supernatural, and whatever is said about God is irrational and unintelligible in the sense of being beyond reason. This mystical Christian belief in a hidden God, then, is explicitly that one can simply believe in God without having any knowledge whatever of what one is purporting to believe in. It is enough to accept God at His word: I am that I am.

We are flying pretty high here, so let's get back down to earth. Most Christians have no interest whatsoever in these logical analyses and conundrums. The important thing for them is to *believe*. The question of the logical meaningfulness of what they believe is irrelevant, beside the point. So God is hidden, unknown. So what? Take Jesus for your savior, be born again, and you will abide eternally in paradise with your loved ones.

I do intend to discuss the doctrine of the unknown and unknowable God, but before entering that esoteric realm of thought, let's look at some Christian doctrinal mysteries that are not sheer logical contradictions, but rather are primarily natural impossibilities. The first is the virgin birth of Jesus Christ. Jesus was not conceived in Mary through her intercourse with a man whose sperm fertilized her ovum. It is said that Jesus is the son of God, but obviously God is not the sort of entity that could impregnate Mary in any natural way. The Immaculate Conception of Jesus is thus a biological impossibility.

The Greek gods impregnated women, but those gods were just various kinds of supermen, like comic book heroes. The Christian God causes Mary to produce Jesus miraculously. Because God is all-powerful, he can cause this miracle. In this usage, "miracle" means something that bypasses the laws of nature, as does Mary's Immaculate Conception.

Another miracle is raising someone from the dead, as Jesus did with Lazarus. Jesus himself was raised from the dead three days after dying on the cross. This is biologically impossible. But note also that it is very important to Christianity, in which the resurrection of the bodies of true believers at the end of time is a key doctrine.

Now just as the anti-Trinitarians and anti-mysterians try to purge Christianity of unintelligible doctrines, so do some people argue that there are or can be natural explanations for virgin birth and the raising of the dead. With various biological techniques, an ovum might be stimulated to produce an embryo and a baby without having been fertilized by a sperm. It has been done with frogs. There is even a condition of suspended animation in which people can appear to be dead for a day or more, and then revive. Finally, some heart-attack victims have been revived by electric shock, and it is not beyond possibility that Frankenstein's dream of creating a living being out of parts of cadavers may one day be accomplished.

Most Christians, however, do not welcome or accept natural explanations of miracles or of contradictory or supernatural doctrines. What appeals is the contradictory and supernatural, miraculous content of these doctrines. The miracles are taken to confirm the truth of the religious doctrines themselves. Without the mysteries, there would be no Christianity—as both the followers and opponents of John Toland came to realize.

But enough of that for now. The basic conclusion to be drawn about most ordinary Christian believers is that they do not understand the specific doctrines they believe in because those doctrines are unintelligible and beyond understanding. Believers just believe them, period.

So put aside the problem of how one can believe what one does not understand. Ask instead: why do Christians believe what they do not understand? A common answer is that it gives them comfort and confidence to believe in the doctrines of a religion that promises them eternal life after death if they believe in God, are good, and take Jesus as their Savior. That this makes no logical sense makes no difference to them at all. Concerning those who actually look into the logic of it, my experience is that rather than taking their illogical beliefs to be nonsense, they take all this logic chopping to be nonsense.

How do the strongest advocates of reason—scientists—respond? Let's consider now the views of three prominent American scientists. Culturally, all of them are Christian, but only one of them professes to accept traditional Christian doctrine. All of them witness to their own faith, hope, and belief. I start with Ursula Goodenough, a distinguished biologist who does not purport to believe in Christian doctrine, but who is a Christian in the sense that the culture and practices of Christianity give her solace. If she had been born and raised in a Hindu country, Hinduism might have served her just as well.

Ursula Goodenough favors the notion that God is simply the basic force that maintains the universe (deism), but she seems to wish that she could believe in a personal God (theism). Being culturally a Christian and having many Christian attitudes still leaves her with something to be desired, but in her book *The Sacred Depths of Nature*, she is concerned almost entirely with religious feelings and hardly at all with belief and doctrine. As a scientist, she is a reductionist who believes that everything, including living beings, is at bottom made up of the basic particles of physics: quarks, strings, or whatever. She is also a mechanistic determinist, which means that she believes that everything that happens in the material world, including the behavior and actions of human beings, is determined by natural laws. We may feel that we have free will and that we control our bodies, but in fact everything we do and think is the result of material atoms interacting lawfully under the impetus of the natural gravitational, electromagnetic, and weak and strong atomic forces. Now quickly, let me say (what I will discuss at length below) that this is in perfect accord with Saint Augustine's doctrines about God's absolute power over his creation. It is solid, primary Christian doctrine. God has determined everything that happens in the universe, including everything we do, think, and feel, including the agonies many people have when worrying about whether or not God exists and what to believe about religion. God, on this deterministic view that pervades both Christianity and Western science, determines that I have no religious sentiments, no anxieties about religion, and that even so I am curious about this extremely important and pervasive human phenomenon.

So Ursula Goodenough does not believe in the supernatural in the sense of impossible things existing (no square circles) or contradictory events taking place (no rising from the dead). She does not believe in miracles in the sense of something happening not determined by the laws of nature. But she *does* yearn to feel such religious emotions as

> serious reflection, reverence, gratitude, and penance . . . in the context . . . of a fully modern, up-to-date understanding of Nature. (p. xi)

Her religiosity comes from a primal experience that she describes as follows:

> I've had a lot of trouble with the universe. It began soon after I was told about it in physics class. I was perhaps twenty, and went on a camping trip, where I found myself in a sleeping

18

bag looking up into the crisp Colorado night. Before I could look around for Orion and the Big Dipper, I was overwhelmed with terror. The panic became so acute that I had to roll over and bury my face in my pillow. (p. 9)

Like the seventeenth-century mathematician and scientist Blaise Pascal and many others before her, Goodenough looked into the starry Heavens and was terrified by the infinite spaces. Pascal believed in God so fervently that he believed that Jesus visited him and told him that he was saved. But Goodenough had no faith in God, was not visited by Jesus, and so was thrown into a "bleak emptiness." (p. 10) She pulled herself out of this by focusing on the mystery of it all:

> The Mystery of why there is anything at all, rather than nothing.

> The Mystery of where the laws of physics came from.

> The Mystery of why the universe seems so strange. (p. 11)

Mystery provides no explanation, but:

Mystery generates wonder, and wonder generates awe. The gasp can terrify or the gasp can emancipate. As I allow myself to experience cosmic and quantum Mystery, I join the saints and the visionaries in their experience of what they called the Divine, and I pulse with the spirit, if not the words, of my favorite hymn:

Immortal, invisible, God only wise,
In light inaccessible hid from our eyes,
Most blessed, most glorious, the Ancient of Days,
Almighty, victorious, thy great name we praise.
—Walter Chalmers Smith, 1867 (pp. 11–12)

This places her in the tradition of those who believe in an ineffable, hidden God about Whom we know literally nothing. But even with all this, Goodenough cannot believe in a personal God, nor anything illogical or supernatural. She satisfies her religious needs with awe and reverence for an experience she takes to be of the sacred

Mystery. She says she loves traditional religions, but there is not one word in her book about evil nor even of nature red in tooth and claw. She professes her faith by saying that

> the existence of all this complexity and awareness and intent and beauty, and my ability to apprehend it, serves as the ultimate meaning and the ultimate value. (p. 171)

The panic brought on by the thought that the universe has no meaning is overcome by a feeling of rapture in the face of the Mystery of it all. Ursula Goodenough has been President of the American Society of Cell Biology and of the Institute on Religion in an Age of Science. She attends a Presbyterian Church regularly. Is she a Christian? Keep her position in mind when we get to Pascal.

Let's now consider a fervently believing Christian, Jane Goodall, the famous student of chimpanzees. Goodall moves beyond yearning and feeling to belief in supernatural Christian doctrine. Rather than being terrified by the starry Heavens, she finds her horrors here on earth: the Holocaust, Tutsi and Hutu reciprocal genocide, human overpopulation and destruction of the earth's ecosystem, and even her beloved chimpanzees engaging in cannibalism and gang murder. In *Reasons for Hope: A Spiritual Journey*, she comes to the conclusion that

> There are really only two ways, it seems to me, in which we can think about our existence here on earth. We either agree with Macbeth that life is nothing more than "a tale told by an idiot," a purposeless emergence of life-forms including the clever, greedy, selfish, and unfortunately destructive species that we call *Homo sapiens*—the "evolutionary goof." Or we believe that, as Pierre Teilhard de Chardin put it, "There is something afoot in the universe, something that looks like gestation and birth." In other words, a plan, a purpose to it all.
>
> As I thought about these ultimate questions . . . I personally was utterly convinced that there was a great spiritual power that we call God, Allah, or Brahma, although I knew, equally certainly, that my finite mind could never comprehend its form or nature. (pp. 92–93).

20

Goodall was raised as a Protestant (Methodist) Christian, for whom "God . . . was the Great Spirit in whom 'We live and move and have our being.'" (p. xii) She keeps to this faith in saying that

> I personally have never been afraid of death itself for I have never wavered in believing that part of us, the spirit or the soul, continues on. (p. 152)

Thus, in contrast to Goodenough, Goodall opposes "reductionist, over-simplistic, mechanistic science." (p. 74) But like Goodenough, she too had a primal moment one day in the Congo when she was watching chimpanzees:

> Lost in awe at the beauty around me, I must have slipped into a state of heightened awareness. It is hard—impossible, really—to put into words the moment of truth that suddenly came upon me then. Even the mystics are unable to describe their brief flashes of spiritual ecstasy. It seemed to me, as I struggled afterward to recall the experience, that *self* was utterly absent: I and the chimpanzees, the earth and trees and air, seemed to become one with the spirit power of life itself . . . I had not been visited by the angels or other Heavenly beings that characterize the visions of the great mystics or saints, yet for all that I believe it truly was a mystical experience. (pp. 173–174)

This experience leads Goodall to conclude that

> there are other windows [than those of science] through which we humans can look out into the world around us, windows through which the mystics and the holy men of the East, and the founders of the great world religions, have gazed as they searched for the meaning and purpose of our life on earth, not only the wondrous beauty of the world, but also in its darkness and ugliness . . . I had seen through such a window. In a flash of "outsight" I had known timelessness and quiet ecstasy, sensed a truth of which mainstream science is merely a small fraction. And I knew that the revelation would be with me for the rest of my life, imperfectly

remembered yet always within. A source of strength on which I could draw when life seemed harsh or cruel or desperate. (p. 175)

The world is very cruel and life often desperate for perhaps half the people in the world. Goodall admits to having no comprehension of how her compassionate God could allow so much evil and suffering in the world. But she is optimistic by nature, and believes that despite the fact that humans are causing extinctions of earth's animal and plant life on a scale matched only twice before in all geologic time, humans can and will save the environment and the world.

Unlike Goodenough, who has no doctrinal beliefs, Goodall believes in at least three Christian doctrines: that a personal God exists, that this God is good, and that human souls will survive death. But she also says that she cannot comprehend God, nor, presumably, can she comprehend illogical Christian doctrines.

The experiences of Goodenough and Goodall must be separated from their beliefs. Goodenough's panic attack is not an uncommon human experience, and it is one of the most frightening things a person can experience. A panic attack can be controlled by drugs or, as Goodenough did, even by not thinking about what brought it on. She put it aside by generating another experience, the feeling of Mystery, which she takes to be religious. Also, and I am sure that this helps, she attends a Protestant church and participates fully in its activities, although she does not believe in its doctrines.

But what about experiences such as those Goodall had in the Congo? How do you tell that an experience is mystical? In 1902, William James in *Varieties of Religious Experience* described how experiences deemed mystical or religious can be generated spontaneously by the human brain, or by drugs, fasting, lack of sleep, exposure to cold, sensory deprivation, such as sitting in a dark cave alone for forty-eight hours, or epilepsy. All of the experiences called mystical can be generated by application of these means, something most of the great mystics knew perfectly well and utilized.

What is required to confirm the belief that any of these experiences is religious? And do any of them open windows to knowledge of meanings that exceed the reach of reason, logic, and science? Or of ordinary understanding?

As for whether these experiences are really religious, suppose you hear a voice in your head that says, "This is God speaking. I want you to get out there and kill the President (or John Lennon)." How do you know you are not crazy? Martin Luther and John Calvin thought they had heard from God, but the Catholics argued that they were simply lunatics who were hearing voices. There is the example of Reverend Jones of Jonesville, convinced that God wanted his congregation to commit suicide by drinking poisoned Kool-Aid. The problem is that you have only your own feelings to go on. There is no independent test to determine whether or not the voice in your head really is God's voice. Years ago that problem really bothered my daughter when Abraham set off to sacrifice his son Isaac. How did he know it was God speaking? And then she thought the appearance of the ram was a cop-out.

As for the knowledge or meanings derived from your religious experience, Goodall puts her finger on the problem: "Even the mystics are unable to describe their brief flashes of spiritual ecstasy" (p. 193). I do not want to be mean about this, but I have known potheads who have the same problem. Again, there is no outside check on what you take your religious experience to mean. Nor any assurance that it was not caused by something you ate, drank, or smoked. That you take an experience to be religious, or to have a certain meaning, or to provide you with certain knowledge is not adequate to confirm either that the experience is religious or that it has a certain meaning. Pascal knew this, and it was a source of great anxiety for him, despite his initial assurance that Jesus as God had visited him and that everything was all right, that is, that he was one of the elect and would go to Heaven. He worried about this on his death bed. His last words were: "May God never abandon me!" Well might he be worried, knowing as he did that on the cross Jesus himself said, "My God, my God, why hast Thou forsaken me?"

Goodenough is a deist who believes in God as an impersonal force in the universe. Goodall is a theist who believes in a personal God. Let's turn now to another distinguished scientist who tries to have it both ways. The evolutionary biologist Stephen Jay Gould has resurrected the ancient doctrine of the two truths, one of science, one of religion. He says that science and religion are Non-Overlapping Magisteria (domains of authority in teaching):

> NOMA is a simple, humane, rational, and altogether conventional argument for mutual respect, based on non-overlapping subject matter, between two components of wisdom in a full human life: our drive to understand the factual character of nature (the magisterium of science), and our need to define meaning in our lives and a moral basis for our actions (the magisterium of religion). (p. 175)

> To summarize . . . the net, or magisterium, of science covers the empirical realm: what is the universe made of (fact) and why does it work this way (theory). The magisterium of religion extends over questions of ultimate meaning and moral value. These two magisteria do not overlap. . . . To cite the old clichés, science gets the age of rocks, and religion the rock of ages, science studies how the Heavens go, religion how to go to Heaven. (p. 6)

Gould is espousing the Aristotelian view that there is a distinct method for investigating and knowing about each distinct subject matter. Modern science is based on the break with this tradition made in 1637 by Descartes in his *Discourse on Method*. Gould agrees with Descartes that there is only one method for investigating all factual matters, the stars as well as the earth, biology as well as physics. Gould then goes on to claim that because science is about facts, and religion is about ultimate meaning and moral values, science and religion constitute two separate realms of subject matter and knowledge, and thus do not conflict with one another. The problem with this (as Gould knows perfectly well) is that some scientific facts and religious doctrines contradict one another. To take an example from Christianity, transubstantiation in the Eucharist requires that the body and blood of Christ be both vastly extended in quantity, and in many places at the same time. These manifestations are physically impossible, so any statement that they happen is factually false. As religious doctrine, however, transubstantiation is true in the religious domain. Gould has to know this, so he is just willfully ignoring the Christian doctrine of transubstantiation, probably because he agrees with John Toland that Christianity—or religion as he conceives of it—cannot or should not be mysterious, that is, Gould simply does not take seriously the professed contradictory and irrational beliefs of Christian believers.

The doctrine of two truths that Gould revives has long been denied as heresy by both Catholics and Protestants. But for most religions, there is a separate religious truth, to which rational or factual truth must accommodate. Descartes himself got in trouble with the Catholic Church by giving physical explanations of transubstantiation. He backed off by saying that although science and religion appear to conflict, they do not, but how they are reconciled with one another is a mystery humans cannot comprehend. Then he stayed away from problems of religious doctrine and concentrated on his studies in physics, physiology, and psychology.

Gould does not remark on the historical background of the two-truths doctrine, nor does he point out that the advancement of science since the seventeenth century derives from its denial. As religion requires that science subordinate itself to religion, science requires that religion itself is a subject of science. Nothing, not even ultimate meanings and moral values, is exempt from scientific investigation. And the more scientists have learned about the way the world and human beings work, the less they have believed (or even claimed to comprehend) such contradictory religious doctrines as those of the Trinity, Immaculate Conception, Resurrection from the dead, the duality of Christ as both human and Divine, and the Eucharist. All world religions are based on miracles that are physical or logical contradictions. The traditional conflict between science and religion lies precisely in the difference between rational belief in empirically tested and confirmed non-contradictory scientific facts on the one hand, and on the other hand, irrational belief in doctrines that cannot be tested and thus cannot be confirmed or disconfirmed. The difference is not—as Gould claims—between subject matters of fact for science and of ultimate meanings and moral values for religion, but rather is between the rational foundational principles of science and the irrational foundational doctrines of religion.

The reason Gould does not find that science and religion conflict is because he ignores religious doctrines that conflict with science. He simply dismisses, for example, the claims of creationists in their arguments against Darwinian evolution (he says in effect that he has better things to do than debate with nuts), and then he chastises some scientists who generalize about religion:

> [There are] among my own scientific colleagues, some militant atheists whose blinkered concept of religion grasps none of the subtlety or diversity, and equates this entire magisterium with the silly and superstitious beliefs of people who think they have seen a divinely crafted image of the Virgin in the drying patterns of morning dew on the plate-glass window of some auto showroom in New Jersey. (p. 69)

In such a statement, Gould ignores and dismisses (and shows his scorn for) the fact that basic doctrines of Christianity (and other religions) involve miracles wrought by divine crafting (for example, Immaculate Conception) that are thought by most scientists, including Gould I am sure, to be just as silly as the auto showroom virgin. If any religious doctrine covers the same subject matter as biology, Virgin Birth is it.

Gould speaks of miracles and religious dogma as "insults to the human intellect" (p. 209), and says that miracles, which he defines as "a unique and temporary suspension of natural law to reorder the facts of nature by divine fiat," cannot happen (p. 85). Finally, he attacks organized religion, which he says

> has fostered throughout Western history . . . the most unspeakable horrors . . . [as a result of] the frequent confluence of religion with secular power. (p. 9)

He thinks all will be fine if we deprive religious leaders of secular power and get scientists and religious leaders to sit down together to discuss the realms of fact and value. They, being "people of goodwill and keen intellect" (p. 8), will agree to leave factual matters to science, and moral problems and the meaning of life to religion. He appears (or pretends) to be ignorant of the fact that the Muslim religion is doctrinally a state religion that covers both religious and secular matters. Catholicism also ruled over the secular as well as the divine until the seventeenth century, and still would if it had the power.

Gould is a distinguished and important scientist whose views probably represent those of many scientists who simply cannot take religion seriously. He seems oblivious to two major doctrines of most world religions. The first is the belief that the human soul is separate from, and survives the death of, the human body. The second is a set of beliefs about how one should act in this life to assure the salvation of one's soul. The great difficulty—which Gould does not take to be a serious problem—is that religions differ concerning what one must believe and how one must behave to attain salvation. There are contradictory beliefs on this matter even among different Christian denominations. This gives rise to the major question all theists who believe in a personal God should ask. It is a factual question. Which is the true religion? or, Which is the true God? It is not a question that can be answered within the domain of religion, for all religions purport to be the true one, the one whose followers worship the true God.

It is important to recognize that questions *about* religious matters are factual. Factual questions can be very difficult to answer. For example, in the seventeenth century, it was pointed out that even if the Pope were infallible, no one else was, so only the Pope could know for certain who the Pope was, or even if they did, they could not be sure they understood what he said.

The point is that it is reasonable to think that one must use scientific (that is, factual) techniques to try to determine which is the true religion. This is because rational methods are required to understand what religious doctrines mean. But this understanding is impossible to accomplish with certainty, which leads to the anguish felt by people who are truly concerned to believe in the true religion so as to save their souls. This is a terrifying problem even for people who have no doubt whatsoever that a personal God exists. They are driven to ask: the God of which faith? This anguished state of mind is obviously one in which Gould does not find himself, nor does he think any intelligent person is going to get worked up about which religion to follow to appease the true God. Descartes was ecumenical to the extent that he stressed that Jews, Christians, and Muslims all worship the same God, and that Protestants and Catholics go to the same Heaven.

Most religious believers will not accept the claim that one can or must use factual and scientific methods to determine which is the true religion. They say that one does not discover the true religion by reasoning and scientific investigation, but by faith, which is irrational. Evangelical Christians believe that Catholics and non-Evangelical Protestants—let alone Jews and Muslims, who have not been Born Again and taken Jesus Christ as their Savior—will be swallowed up in the fires of Hell. This is graphically described in *Glorious Appearing*, the twelfth volume of the *Left Behind* series of Evangelical Protestant novels by Tim La Haye and Jerry B. Jenkins. You might object to my citing this pot-boiler series, but any set of twelve religious novels that is translated into dozens of languages and has sold hundreds of millions copies must be taken seriously.

Gould ignores the wild, fantastic beliefs given expression in such writings as the *Left Behind* series. "Left Behind" refers, as most readers probably know, to the bulk of humankind that is left behind when, during the Rapture, God takes up into Heaven the true believers—Born Again Evangelical Christians who are truly sincere in their belief. But even for non-Evangelical Christians, if you are to be a Christian, you must believe utterly that Christ died for your sins. If you are a Muslim, you must agree that Mohammed set down the rules for secular behavior as well as for religious belief. The great difficulty is that there is no way to arbitrate among religions, each of which is based on dogmatic claims of unique access to Divine authority.

The criterion of religious Truth—Divine authority—is dependent on the personal convictions (the faith) of religious leaders and believers within each religion. In contrast, all factual claims to knowledge are arbitrated by the same publicly observable tests. But there is no way to adjudicate between the faith or authoritative convictions of one religion and those of another. Each religion—and each sect of each religion—claims absolute authority to know the absolute Truth.

This mutual exclusiveness of the religious Truths of different religions explains why intolerance between religions is as strong as or even stronger than that between religion and science. Conflicts between religions, let alone between religion and science, are not open to negotiation or truce. Members of each religion are absolutely certain that theirs is the True religion. Thus European Christians mounted the Crusades to convert the heathen Muslims, and the Muslim Turks drove deep into Europe to convert the heathen Christians. This particular battle is not over, and seems set to dominate the twenty-first century.

I conclude this discussion of three distinguished scientists' views of religion by commenting that Gould's view of religion is as narrow and naive as the views of Goodenough and Goodall. Science allows only rational, naturalistic truths. Religion makes claims for irrational supernatural truths, and many of these religious doctrines conflict with scientific facts. Goodenough is perfectly satisfied with this conclusion because for her religion amounts operationally to personal therapy. Goodall finds religion to be exhilarating, she has faith in the promise of an after-life, and she glorifies in mystical experience. Gould simply cannot take the irrational, supernatural, contradictory doctrines of religion seriously. He cannot conceive that anyone actually believes in miracles, or accepts as meaningful, statements that are literal contradictions, such as that Jesus Christ is both Divine and human. But many people do have such beliefs. Finally, none of the three addresses the issue of the power over believers exercised by organized religion. Finally, if Gould truly believed that religious leaders would willingly give up any interest in secular political power, he would have to be abysmally naive or ignorant about both human nature and religion.

Saint Thomas Aquinas points out that none of the proposed proofs for the existence of God actually proves that God exists. He presents some of them simply to bolster the faith of believers. As examples, I discuss three major proofs for the existence of God both to exhibit their appeal and to show how they fail.

First, the ontological proof for the existence of God. It is very simple. Among God's perfections is necessary existence. Not just existence, for all sorts of things exist. But God exists necessarily, that is, God cannot not exist. The reason is that if God could not exist, then God would not be God. For God is all-powerful, and if it were possible for God not to exist, then God would not be all-powerful. Thus God necessarily exists.

A general objection to this proof proposed by Immanuel Kant is that existence is not a property or a characteristic or a feature of God, nor of anything else. Something either exists or does not exist, but to say that a thing exists or not is not to say anything about what it is. So just because God is perfect does not mean that God exists, because existence is not a property and thus not a perfection.

Not everyone accepts this criticism of the ontological argument. So let's look at another version.

A proof for the existence of God based on the notion that God is infinite has long been persuasive and attractive to believers. Part of its attraction, for Descartes, for example, is that it also constitutes an attack on Aristotle. Aristotle said that there is nothing in the understanding that was not first in the senses. This means that every idea in our minds has to be derived from our sensory experiences. Even general ideas, such as the concept of the number four, has to be derived from seeing such things as four apples, four tomatoes, and so on. This view is called Empiricism because all of our ideas, even the most general ones, are said to be based on empirical experience.

Where, then, philosophers such as Descartes ask, does our idea of infinity come from? We can build up from our knowledge of particular things, apples, for example, numbers of enormous magnitude, but we cannot generate an infinite number. Yet, we do have an idea of infinity. This idea in our understanding was *not* derived from something that we first experienced in our sensible experience, so it must have come from somewhere else. Philosophers who hold this view—that we have at least one idea that is *not* derived from sensible experience—are called Rationalists.

So where did the idea of infinity come from? We cannot experience it. So how can we finite human beings think of infinity? Descartes reasoned that our idea of infinity must have been put in our minds by something that is actually infinite. And lo, we do have in our minds an idea of a God who is infinitely powerful, all knowing, infinitely good, in a word, an infinite God. We have no direct sensible experience of this God, and so (Descartes said) the only way we could have an idea of infinity is if this infinite God directly placed an idea of Himself in our minds. Thus because we have an idea in our minds of an infinite God that we could never directly experience, this God must have put the idea of His Infinite Self in our minds: therefore God exists. God exists because we cannot make up ideas just out of nothing. Our ideas must have actually existing causes. They must either be derived from our sensory experience, or placed in our minds by something that actually exists. Thus, because we have an idea of infinity, God exists.

Since Descartes's time, mathematicians have postulated—had ideas of—a vast number of things that no one has ever experienced, or ever can experience empirically through the senses. Such things as pi, negative numbers, and matrices or spaces of as many dimensions (physicists today talk of eleven strings) as they wish to think about. Not imagine: one can *imagine* only the three-dimensional space one has sensory experiences of. But you can *conceive* of all sorts of mathematical spaces and entities that you cannot perceive.

So where did all these ideas of non-sensible things come from? You could say that they come from God, that God gives us these general mathematical ideas—just as He gave us the idea of infinity—and this proves that God exists. This is certainly the strongest rational argument—as opposed to just feeling it—that God exists. But it does not work. Here is why.

Suppose there is a realm of non-sensible, non-empirical entities that we can encounter to obtain all kinds of non-experiential mathematical ideas, including the idea of infinity. Plato believed that there is such a realm. But even the existence of such a non-experiential realm of ideas does not prove that God exists. It just shows that we can get ideas from a source other than sensible experience. There is nothing in this proposal that proves that the cause of these non-empirical or non-experiential ideas must be God.

To make this obvious, I now consider the most common proof for the existence of God, the cosmological proof. This is a very simple proof that also involves the idea of infinity. It depends on one of the first principles in the development of Western Philosophy, the maxim: Something cannot come from nothing. That is, everything must have a cause. So never mind what our world is like, it must have been created by something. There must be a first cause. A lot of people accept this argument.

Descartes gives a homely example of it. He says that he came from his parents and they came from their parents, but that line could not go on infinitely. Somewhere there had to be a first cause, and that is God.

But there is a very serious problem. If everything needs a cause, what caused God?

There is a philosophical joke about this. An Indian holy man is asked what holds up the earth. The earth rests on the back of an elephant. But what does the elephant stand on? A turtle. What holds up the turtle? It is, the wise man says, turtles all the way down.

You can interpret this to mean that there is no first cause, which goes against the principle you started with. But if there is no first cause, then you cannot prove that God exists as the first cause. But you do not want to deny that God is the first cause. Well, the Bible says there is a first cause, and this cause is God. God created the Heavens and the earth.

But I have already raised the logical problem caused by God having to exist so He can bring Himself into existence. Thus the cosmological argument that God must exist to be the first cause fails because it depends on the logically fallacious circular argument that God must exist before He exists so He can bring Himself into existence.

But suppose God is not in time. Then it might seem that in an a-temporal context, God could cause Himself to exist. But cause and effect make sense only in temporal sequence.

The argument that God exists as the first cause of the universe thus collapses.

The third argument for the existence of God is the design argument. The eighteenth-century theologian William Paley gave the following version of the design argument. Suppose you find a watch on a heath. Where did it come from? Obviously, if there is a watch, there was a watchmaker. Now consider the universe. It is infinitely more complex in design than a watch. So there must be a universe maker. The problem with this argument from analogy—watch is to watch maker as universe is to universe maker—is that you can check to see if there is a watch maker, but you cannot check to see if there is a universe maker. So while the argument is suggestive, it can never be confirmed.

But, the eighteenth-century philosopher David Hume said, let's go along with the design argument and see where it leads. Assume that God did make the world. But God is good, so why is the world in such a mess? Hume postulated that maybe our God is senile and has been delegated to the edge of the universe so he can fuss around making a mess where it doesn't matter much. Or maybe our God is an infant God Who is being allowed to play in a sandbox area of the universe until He grows up enough to make a decent world. Finally, Hume proposed the worst of all possible situations: Maybe our God is a Committee.

Hume is something of a humorist, but his point is serious. He argues that the presence of evil in the universe rules out the existence of God, or at least it rules out the existence of an infinitely good God.

Nevertheless, the argument from design is the most popular argument for the existence of God in America today. It is also the weakest. It is proposed by Evangelical Christians who until quite recently depended on the creationist view that there had to be a Creator—a first cause—of the universe. The logical arguments against the first cause argument—as befits true believers—did not bother them at all. What does bother them is the fact that the U.S. Constitution calls for the separation of church and state, and so Creationism cannot be taught in American schools. So now they propose the argument from Intelligent Design. The universe is so complex, they say, that it could not have evolved from random movements of particles thrown out by the Big Bang, but must have been designed by an intelligent entity. They carefully do not say that this entity is God, but Who else could it be?

How about highly intelligent extraterrestrial beings from another galaxy that seeded our planet with life? Yes, but where did *they* come from?

The argument from Intelligent Design instantly raises the question: Who designed the designer? If the universe is so complex it needs a designer, the designer must be even more complex than the universe, so the designer needs a designer, and so on. Turtles all the way down.

Whether you pursue this line of argument through an infinite regress, or back to a first cause, it collapses. Again, that this point is virtually never raised in encounters between the proponents of Intelligent Design and their opponents is a measure of how little these arguments—either *for* or *against* the existence of God—actually matter to true believers.

Consequently, I apologize for taking your time discussing arguments for (and against) the existence of God. Believers do not need them and unbelievers do not heed them.

The existence of God is accepted on faith as a mystery.

I will get to the mystery, but first I outline the foundational doctrines of traditional Christianity that are taken from the Bible as interpreted by Saint Augustine. I am quite aware that other than by some Calvinists, Saint Augustine's interpretation is fully accepted by virtually no Christians today—neither by Evangelical Protestants nor by Catholics. So you should be aware that almost all believers, ministers and priests, and theologians and professors of religion will say, as some of them have said to me: Nobody believes that Augustinian stuff today. But the issue is not how many people believe it today, but whether or not the interpretation is correct. Even theologians who dismiss it agree that Saint Augustine's interpretation of Christian doctrine is the most straightforwardly solid and historically grounded interpretation. It is by no means the most comforting interpretation, and thus it is not the most likely to attract and hold believers. This is one reason why Saint Thomas and the fathers of the Catholic Church have abandoned Augustinianism. They have separated the issue of interpretation from the issue of orthodoxy. The orthodox doctrines of Christianity today have been chosen because they are simpler and easier to understand, and are less contradictory than, the Augustinian interpretation. For example, you will not learn from either Protestant ministers or Catholic priests that taking Jesus as your Savior is not a simple matter of just believing, and that it is literally impossible. But if one is to face the true challenge of Christianity, one must contend with Saint Augustine who says that because everything is caused by God, you can have faith only if God causes you to have faith, you can choose Jesus as your Savior only if God causes you to choose Jesus as your Savior. This is the hard core of God's direct and intimate relationship to human beings.

The reason that neither most Protestants nor the Catholic Church adhere today to strict Augustinian Christianity is because in the sixteenth century, the Catholics recognized that Augustinian Christianity is so severe that ordinary believers, not to mention kings, queens, and noblemen, could not be expected to adhere to its stringencies. So to save the Church, the Catholics, particularly the Jesuits in the seventeenth century, cut down on Augustinian rigor and severity in favor of the more relaxed views of Saint Thomas Aquinas concerning salvation. And these relaxed views led to the simple relationship of humans with God professed by present-day Evangelical Christianity.

But first, the weakening and softening of Augustinian orthodoxy in the Catholic Church led to the Protestant Revolution, those disassociations from the Catholic Church by Luther and Calvin. The major point of dissension concerns whether salvation can be attained only through God's gratuitous gift of grace as Augustine, Luther, and Calvin believe, or through human actions of worship and good works as Pelagius (circa A.D. 400) claims. The so-called Pelagian heresy slowly evolved into Church doctrine, but the Lutherans did not accept the view that one can earn salvation until the late twentieth century, and strict Calvinists still maintain the Augustinian position that salvation (and damnation) are predetermined by God independently of human behavior and belief—which behavior and belief, remember, causes problems because it also is fully determined by God.

In more detail and completeness than in the discussions above, then, the Augustinian doctrine of the Christian God involves the following: God is an infinite, omnipotent, omniscient, omni-good, perfect, supernatural spirit. God is *causa sui*, that is, God created Himself. There was nothing, and then God created Himself, and He also created the universe out of nothing. It follows that God is the direct and only cause of everything that is in the universe, and of everything that happens in the universe. Thus God is not only the creative force that brings the universe into existence, and, most importantly, continuously keeps the universe in existence through that creative force, God is also the designer of the universe and the deterministic cause, force, or power that determines and maintains

35

the actions and behavior of everything in the universe. He also determines all of everyone's beliefs, a point that I have already mentioned bedeviled Pascal. Whether one conceives of the ongoing universe as proceeding or existing in discrete moments, or as existing continuously through seamless time, God is the creative force, the causal power that makes everything in the universe exist, be what it is, and do what it does. Because of this, everything is what it is necessarily, and does what it does necessarily. Again, people and things in the universe have no freedom to be what they are or to do what they do. Everything is determined, in fact predetermined, by God's infinite power of creation. Nothing has any freedom but God. Thus the universe is a totally deterministic machine. The universe is natural—as opposed to supernatural—in the sense that it proceeds according to laws of nature themselves created by God. Thus the universe and all things in it including human beings are determined in all their movements and beliefs by God.

It follows that in being omnipotent, God is also omniscient. God knows everything about the universe prior to its creation—because God creates it. From the beginning—really before the beginning— God knows everything that has happened, is happening, and will happen. But although God creates the universe and determines and knows all that happens in the universe, God himself is not a part of this universe, nor does God exist in time or in space. God is an eternal, infinite, all-knowing, designing, creating, maintaining, non-temporal, non-spatial, supernatural being. He is supernatural in the sense that He is a spiritual being above, and not a part of, the natural world of which we are a part. In contrast to the material universe, God is a conscious person.

Human beings are among God's creations. The first man was Adam and the first woman Eve. God gave them free will, the ability to make their own choices. God placed them in the Garden of Eden, and forbade Adam only one thing. He was not to eat fruit from the Tree of the Knowledge of Good and Evil. But Adam chose to disobey God by eating from the Tree. Consequently, God banished Adam and Eve from the Garden of Eden, and put a curse on all Adam's progeny. Thus to the present day, all human beings are born in sin, they have a propensity to sin and evil, they do not have free will, and thus neither can they choose to do good nor can they do good. They are determined to choose and engage in concupiscence, that is, material pleasures, all of which are sinful, and to turn their backs on spiritual goodness and God.

God, however, took mercy on humankind (this is the Christian part of Christianity) and sent Jesus Christ, His only begotten Son, to earth to preach salvation and to die on the cross for humankind. But human beings, still cursed by the Fall of Man, (Saint Paul, Romans 5:12–21) cannot chose Jesus as their Savior without the help of grace given by God. God gives this grace gratuitously without any consideration of anyone's behavior. None of sinning humankind deserves grace, none can earn it. The behavior of everyone, anyway, is necessarily sinful because since the Fall of Man everyone is born in sin and has inclinations only toward evil thoughts and behavior.

Because of Adam's disobedience and the consequent Fall of Man, God owes us nothing (which, *God Owes Us Nothing*, is a quotation from Pascal and the title of a most excellent book on Pascal and Augustinian Jansenism by Leszek Kolakowski, to which I am indebted). God's grace, which causes us to have belief in God and to worship God, is gratuitous. Moreover, and this is crucial to Augustinian Christianity, whether anyone is saved or damned is predetermined by God in His conception of and creation of the world. This is the doctrine of Predestination. Before anyone is born (and before Adam and Eve were created), God predetermines for each and every human being who will ever live, who will be saved and who will be damned. How human beings behave has nothing whatsoever to do with whether one is saved or damned. This follows quite logically from the fact that the Fall of Man means that no human being thereafter has free will, and none can choose good over evil because all are born with a propensity to evil. Even those who are awarded grace by God, and thus become true believers who no longer sin, even they cannot *earn* salvation. This again is perfectly logical because the fact that they have (after grace) true belief and do good works does not derive from their free choices—they have no free will and so can make no free choices—but is determined as a gift from God. Whether a person goes through life a totally wicked sinner, or whether a person is given grace by God and thus becomes pious and good, is no doing of that person, but is totally determined by God. All human behavior is totally determined by God. So in fact, God has no criteria with which to pick those who are to be saved from those who are to be damned. Thus given the fact that God does save some humans and damn others, it makes perfect logical sense for Him to choose the saved and the damned arbitrarily, without any reference to how they behave in this life—for God Himself determines that behavior. Again, sinful humans have no free will and thus have no control of anything they believe or do. This doctrine of Predestination is at the heart of Augustinian Christianity.

Beginning in the sixteenth century, the increasing laxity of the Catholic hierarchy led more and more to support of the anti-Augustinian (strictly speaking, Pelagian after its primary proponent) doctrine that humans do not need God's grace, but can by their own efforts overcome the curse of Adam, attain faith, and through belief and good works earn their way to salvation. As remarked above, this laxity led Luther and Calvin to break from the Catholic Church. Like Augustine, Luther and Calvin believed that post-lapsarian (after the Fall of Man) human beings are entirely at the mercy of an absolutist God Who creates them, predetermines them to sin, and arbitrarily assigns them to either salvation or damnation.

It is a hard doctrine. I agree with the interpretation of Luther and Calvin that according to Christian doctrine about God, it is impossible for human beings to have free will. Because God is the creating, determining cause of everything that exists and happens, God determines all the behavior of all human beings. Thus even before Adam sinned by disobeying God, Adam could not have had free will. This follows from the fact that the omnipotent God created everything in the universe and determined prior to creation how everything in the universe would act and be. So all Adam's actions were determined from—even before—the instant of creation. Neither the notion of free will nor the notion of human choice of actions makes any sense in such a predetermined universe. So—as my daughter at an early age instantly saw—it makes no sense for God to punish Adam for Adam's behavior, because God made Adam and determined Adam's behavior. Because he had no free will, Adam could not sin. In fact, Adam could not *do* anything. All of his choices and actions were predetermined by God. So it makes no sense to praise or blame Adam for anything he does. Adam's eating the apple would be a sin only if it were Adam's free choice to disobey God. But everything Adam does is determined by God.

In fact, of course, God also determines what is and is not a sin. God chose to punish Adam for disobedience, but He could just as well have chosen to award disobedience to His commands. But God determined that Adam disobeys, and thus sins. But again, it makes no sense to talk either of obeying or disobeying, or to call Adam's action a choice. Adam has no choice. God determines him to act and think the way he does. God is the only active being in the universe, the only being who can act according to His own will. All of God's creation (including his creature Adam and all of Adam's progeny—that's us) is passive. We are not actors, we are puppets, going through the motions and thinking the thoughts and feeling the passions that God has determined that we do, think, and feel. God pulls our strings.

Consequently, our sense that we are free to choose and to act is a delusion and a deception, which also is placed in us by God. We may think and feel that we have free choice and can control our actions, but this is just an illusion imposed on us by God. The bottom-line conclusion from this is that we are not active, causal agents at all. Everything about us, all our thoughts and feelings, our sense of considering and deciding and then acting in this way rather than that way, is a charade. Ultimately it comes to the conclusion that we are not in any way independent or autonomous beings. We are shadow figures projected on a screen by light shining on the formative hand of our Maker.

Obviously, not every Christian notices all these problems stemming from Christian doctrine, or traces them all the way through, but something many Christians have complained or worried about is that it makes no sense to punish Adam's progeny for something Adam did and they did not do. None of that progeny even existed when Adam sinned. You and I did not disobey God by eating the apple from the Tree. A feeling for fairness that seems inborn—and on the doctrine of the omnipotent creating God certainly would have to have been implanted by God—makes everyone indignant at being blamed and punished for something someone else did. But because God causes everything, God causes us to feel this indignation, too, which, when one thinks about it, seems to be a particularly nasty trick. God makes us feel that we should be blamed and punished, praised and rewarded, only for our own thoughts and actions, not for those of someone else, ancestor though he be. But in fact, our thoughts are caused by God, and are our own only in the sense that we have them.

The Christian God also would be causing me to write what I am now writing. If I feel indignant, God makes me feel indignant.

Perhaps (or rather, obviously) God wants people to know about His absolute determinism. Also, of course, He makes it sinful for us to complain.

Saint Augustine simply accepts the logical conclusion that Predestination, that is, total determinism of human behavior, follows from God's omnipotence and omniscience. If this goes against human intuitions about fairness and just desserts, so be it. (God causes humans to have such intuitions.) But never mind. True believers accept the story of the Fall of Man because it is in the Bible.

Later scholars and theologians have tried to avoid Augustine's conclusions by pointing out that his belief that the Bible is the literal word of God came before modern historical and textual studies that show that the Bible is a compilation of different and sometimes contradictory texts chosen by Church fathers for a number of sometimes inconsistent reasons. Thus, they say, many texts Augustine took literally must be taken allegorically, not literally.

But Augustine knew perfectly well about the compilations, inconsistencies, and contradictions in the Bible. Also he understood the notion of allegory. He *still* took the Bible as the literal word of God.

So did Pascal. Like many other thinkers, Pascal was struck—one might say thunder-struck—by his intuition that the Fall of Man is the only explanation that makes any sense of the human condition. Why are human beings so miserable? Why are human beings so prone to evil actions? Why are human beings such nasty pieces of business? David Hume said that man is a scourge to man, and Thomas Hobbes saw every human being as at war against every other human being. The Fall of Man explains it. One reason Christians oppose the Darwinian theory of the survival of the fittest is that it provides the only reasonable and natural explanation for the mean and vicious behavior of human beings other than the Fall of Man.

The story of the Fall of Man is an obvious mess. Why speak of Adam disobeying God when Adam is a puppet with no free will? Why accept these contradictions? Augustine did so because he took the Bible as God's word. The only conclusion from the contradictions—those stemming from God's total creation of the universe and those involved in the miracles—is to say that God is beyond our comprehension. God is a hidden God (Isaiah 45:16). God is ineffable. God is infinite and we are finite so we can never understand God. Because we are imperfect and finite, we can have no concept of the perfect and infinite God.

This raises a most serious question about God. If all we can say about God is that He exists, what are we saying? Existence is not a feature or characteristic or property of God, the way omnipotence, omniscience, etc. are. No matter what characteristics you include in the description of a thing, you cannot derive the existence of that thing from the description of that set of characteristics alone. You have to examine the world to see whether or not it exists. Existence is just the actual being of something that has a set of characteristics, which comes down to saying simply that existence is existence. To say that an entity is infinite, for example, is just to say that it has the characteristic of infinity—it is just part of the entity's description, it proves nothing about whether or not that entity exists.

Because the characteristics of a thing are properties of a thing, and existence is not a property, to say that God exists is to say nothing about the nature of God. But Augustine says a great deal about the characteristics of God. And although it obviously makes no sense to say that our belief, worship, and good works that are the result of God gratuitously giving us Grace count toward our salvation, nevertheless, along the way to weakening these hard-core doctrines, Catholics started promulgating the view that those who are given Grace *do* merit salvation, never mind the contradiction that God predetermines who is saved without consideration of their beliefs and behavior. On their way to weakening the doctrine of Predestination, the Catholics said that although God predetermines the fate of all human beings long before they exist, and even if every human action is determined, even so, if you live a good life, strive not to sin, and pray, God will take mercy and you will go to Heaven. Again, given the hard-core doctrine of Predestination as exposed by Saint Augustine, this makes no sense whatsoever.

Before Augustine became a Christian, he was a Manichean. Manicheans believe that there are two gods of virtually equal power, one good and one evil. Later through sheer strength of will and intellect—or by God's grace—Augustine became a Christian.

Augustine had been a Manichean because of the problem of evil. The Christian God is omni-good, so where does the evil in the universe come from? It can come only from God. So is God evil? One attempt to avoid the conclusion that God is evil is to say that humans cause evil in the world. But God creates all humans, so that will not work.

Some theologians and philosophers say that what we view as evil is from God's viewpoint good. I once heard a prominent Catholic philosopher give a paper defending that view. In the question period someone asked, "Do you mean to say that for God, the Holocaust is good?" "Yes," was the reply. Our finite intellects are just incapable of understanding how this is the case.

Could something be good from God's viewpoint and evil from our viewpoint? Or, given that God decrees what is good and what is evil, might it be the case that from God's viewpoint, a thing or action in itself is neither good nor evil? But this would just add another difficulty about the doctrine of the Fall of Man, because if what is good or evil is determined merely by God's whim or decree, and is neutral in itself, this means again that it is just a charade for God to curse Adam and humankind for disobeying God, when God could just as well have made disobedience the good choice and obedience the sinful or evil choice.

Another suggestion about evil is that it is not something, it is nothing. On this view, evil is not a positive characteristic, but is merely the lack of good. But how, in this view, could evil—which is nothing—be bad? It is not even a characteristic. The notion that evil is just lack of good makes even less sense than the notion that evil from the human standpoint is good from God's standpoint.

The usual Christian way out is just to say the God is good, and the problem of evil is beyond our comprehension.

This problem of how evil can exist in the world when its Creator, God, is omni-good, particularly given the events of the twentieth century, is one of the most difficult sticking points for Christian (and Jewish) believers. One solution is to say that evil is the work of the fallen angel Satan, not the work of God. But the old problem of Adam eating from the Tree of the Knowledge of Good and Evil arises again. For what Satan does is determined by God Who created Satan. So Satan cannot be blamed for evil.

These problems about the omni-good Christian God make Manicheanism seem very reasonable. The notion of two powers—one good, one evil—has great appeal in a world where there is so much evil. I often introduced Manicheanism to students by discussing the *Star Wars* movies, in which there is a force that is sought after and fought over (and with) by the proponents of good (Obi-wan Kenobi) and the proponents of evil (Darth Vader). The twist is that the Christ figure (Luke Skywalker) is the son of the evil god, not the son of the good god.

There is inevitably a religion of devil worshippers, the Yezidis. Devil worshippers reason that there is no point in worshipping God, given that God is good and wishes only the best for humankind. Better to worship and appease the Devil, who is evil and can harm you if you get on his wrong side. This is, however, simplistic, given that the Christian God has a long record of doing bad as well as good things to human beings. You do not need two gods to account for good and evil. The Christian God is adequate for both.

The upshot is that to be an Augustinian Christian—or just to be a conventional theist who believes that God is a person, omniscient, omnipotent, omni-good, and so on—one must accept many incomprehensible and contradictory doctrines on faith. Many people do.

I remark above that I was raised as a Methodist. A major founder of Methodism, John Wesley, was a severe taskmaster, but Methodism in America has been stripped of any serious consideration of the problems discussed above. As I think about it now, all I can revive from Sunday School classes and sermons is the assurance that we are all sinners, but if we believe in God and take Jesus as our savior, and not do anything too awful, we will go to Heaven.

And God's eye is on the sparrow. Over the years, by the way, that quotation (of which I am very fond) has greatly puzzled most of the students in my classes.

There was nothing about being born again in my Methodist Sunday School, which is a requirement of the most powerful religious movement in America today: Evangelical Christianity. One baptism was, and still is, enough for Methodists.

As for the Evangelical requirement that one must be born again, so far as I can discover, the basic (and sure) way to Heaven is simply to take Jesus Christ as your Savior and be baptized, presumably for the second time. Yes, we are born sinners, the Evangelicals agree. But no, our fate after death is not predestined. We can assure our place in Heaven by being born again. No less than former U.S. President Bush (the younger) is a born-again Evangelical Christian. Politicians in the USA notoriously profess being religious, whether they are believers or not, but I believe that President Bush is a true believer. True believers generally believe that they know the Truth, and thus they act with great conviction. Because God is with them, they can impose the Truth on nonbelievers.

Back to basics. A friend and believer said to me something like the following:

> Will you lay off all those contradictions? Who cares? Of course "square circle" is a contradiction, but the fact is that everybody knows what it means. Just because "square circle" is a contradiction does not mean that it is meaningless. And just because you can generate all sorts of contradictions out of the attributes of God, this does not mean that the term "God" is meaningless. Everybody knows what "God" means. So what if it turns out that God's creating Himself means that he has to exist before he exists? That may be a contradiction, but you know what? Everyone understands it. That's a pretty neat trick, creating yourself.

Now I have to be careful here. The easiest rebuttal is to point out that of course we understand each of the two words in "square circle," and we recognize that they contradict one another, but just because "square" and "circle" have meaning, this does not mean that the entire phrase "square circle" has meaning, because it does not. It refers to nothing.

My believer friend says:

> Bah. Look, I know that you want to say that the question "Does God exist?" makes no sense because the very concept of God is contradictory. Concerning God's creating himself, you want to say that because it is a circular fallacy to say "A causes B, and B causes A," that sentence has no meaning. But it does too have meaning, because you have to understand what it means to argue that it is a contradiction.

So again I plod along pointing out that, "A causes B" is understandable, and "B causes A" is understandable, but the two joined together cancel each other out in a contradiction that has no meaning.

Sigh. I am going to lose believers who are interested in my commentary if I continue on that line. So let's say, OK, we all understand what it means to say that God exists. The question then is: How can one determine that the statement "God exists" is true or false? That's really at the heart of this investigation into the notion and existence of God.

For almost all questions having to do with whether or not something exists, we appeal to common sense and sensory experience. In science and philosophy, this is codified as the time-honored empirical meaning criterion, according to which, a statement is meaningful only if one can describe a possible experience that would answer the question of whether the statement is true or false.

> So one might say that we can check to see if there is a square circle in the yard. But if "square circle" is really a meaningless phrase, we would not know what to look for. So the empirical meaning criterion could be used to rule out sentences that make no sense because they contain meaningless phrases. "Square circle" is a contradiction, it has no meaning. But I am told again:

> You yourself are arguing in a circle. You are claiming that just because you have never seen a square circle, square circles don't exist. But, you know, people used to say that black swans don't exist, but then someone found a flock of them.

But . . . but the phrase "black swan" is not contradictory, while the phrase "square circle" is contradictory.

Ach!

During all my years of teaching, I have had students who listen to—and often understand—what I say about the problem of contradictory phrases being meaningless, and then they say: "But how can you be *sure* that square circles and other contradictions don't exist? *Anything* is possible."

Alas, the great burden in teaching logic, philosophy, and science is just to explain how it is that just *anything* is *not* possible. A contradictory phrase such as "square circle" does not describe or refer to anything. Ah! But the bright student exclaims:

> Now you are arguing in a circle. You are defining contradictory phrases such as "square circle" as being meaningless, but how do you know? Just because you've never seen one doesn't prove that there aren't such things.

I've gone on like this long enough either for you to agree that contradictory statements and phrases are empty and meaningless, or for you to opt for the mysterious, to side with those who insist that, "Anything is possible!"

So let's look again at the statement "God exists." Most people will say that that statement has meaning, never mind that detailed examination shows that the concept of God is contradictory. Everybody knows what "God exists" means. Many philosophers and theologians have pointed to things that they take to show that God exists. In the Bible are reports by people who have seen or heard God, and there are miracles caused by God, and there is Jesus Christ the Son of God. Or there is the earth and all that is on it, and the starry heavens, all attesting to the handiwork of God. This leads to the question the creationists ask, which is: Where did everything in the universe come from? On the analogy of human engineers and designers, creationists say that the universe and everything in it is too complicated to have evolved naturally. Instead, the universe must have been designed and created by God. For tactical purposes, many creationists deny that they are assuming that the designer and creator must be God, but who else could it be? But the design hypothesis obviously leads to the question of who designed the designer, and who designed the designer of the designer, and so on. To stop an infinite regress of such questions, one is led to a first designer, God, who designs and creates Himself. And we are back to go again.

But rather than looking for evidence that would prove that God exists, one could ask for a description of a situation that would prove that God does not exist. Karl Popper is famous for proposing this task as a way of telling whether or not a proposition or theory is true or false. It is not enough to describe an empirical situation that would prove that a theory or proposition is true. One must also be able to describe a situation that would prove that the theory is false.

There are a number of theories that turn out to be un-falsifiable because they provide an explanation for every possible situation one could imagine. Freudianism is one of these global theories. If you deny it, the therapist can give you a reason why you deny it. No matter what objection you give to the truth of the theory, the theory itself provides an explanation of why you object in that way. Marxism is another such global theory. No matter what happens, a Marxist can show that it happened as a result of capitalist exploitation. Some forms of feminism are also global theories. Whatever happens is a result of paternal domination by males.

The problem with pointing to the existence and glories of the universe as proof for the existence of God is that you can conceive of no thing or situation that would stand as proof that the proposition "God exists" is false. For Christianity, the presence of evil, given that God is all-good, might be taken as evidence that God does not exist. But the answer to that is that what we perceive as evil may really be good in the eyes of God.

The upshot for skeptics is that given that we can conceive of no situation or thing that, if it existed, would stand as evidence that God does not exist, the existence and glories of the universe do not constitute a proof that God does exist.

Well, "Neither does this lack prove that God does not exist," my believing friend concludes. So he continues to have faith in the existence of God, whose nature is beyond comprehension in the sense that the description of God is contradictory, and for Whom there is no empirical test to determine whether or not He does exist.

That God's existence or God's nonexistence would make no difference in any way to our experience of the world makes the theory that God created the universe untestable, so according to the empirical meaning criterion, this theory is not a scientific theory. To be an empirical, scientific, theory, whether God exists or not would have to make a difference in our experience of the world. That it does not is not, however, seen as a bad thing by many believers. William James, for example, in a famous article entitled "The Will to Believe" (which he said later he should have called "The Right to Believe") said that theories and notions of this type about which no conceivable or possible experience could determine whether they are true or false are open to denial or acceptance for any reason whatsoever. If it makes you feel good, helps you get along in life, and does not harm anyone, then you can believe that God exists.

The sticker there is "does not harm anyone."

The empirical meaning criterion is a primary part of common sense, and is the foundation of meaningfulness in the natural sciences, but because it does seem to rule out any way to test by experience whether or not God exists, it has come under extensive attack both by logicians with a theological bent and by philosophers of science who worry about the existential status of theoretical entities (such as quarks and strings) for which no empirical test for determining whether or not they exist seems adequate. In attacks on the empirical meaning criterion, there is one logical trick that believers in God are particularly fond of, and that they take as a killer argument. I discuss it because it has been appealed to so much, and because it is particularly silly.

It is a logical rule that if two propositions are connected by the phrase "and/or," then the combined statement is meaningful if at least one (but not necessarily both) of the two propositions is meaningful. For example, the combined statement "'Grass is green' and/or 'Twas brillig, and the slithy toves, Did gyre and gimble in the wabe'" is meaningful, because "Grass is green" is empirically testable and so is meaningful, even though "Twas brillig, and the slithy toves, Did gyre and gimble in the wabe" is nonsense. This logical rule has actually been proposed by some believers to support the view that "God exists" is meaningful because "'Grass is green' and/or 'God exists'" is meaningful. They make this claim even though in fact "God exists"

48

is not empirically meaningful because it cannot be empirically determined to be either true or false. The simple way around this is to add the requirement that each of the combined sentences must be meaningful alone. The addition of this requirement is warranted by the recognition that it rules out obviously silly results such as the claim that nonsense statements such as "Twas brillig and the slithy toves, Did gyre and gimble in the wabe" are meaningful. I am not insisting here that "God exists" is a nonsense statement (although I do give the standard grounds above for thinking so), but only that the logical rule about the meaningfulness of combined statements connected by "and/or" does not provide grounds for concluding that "God exists" is a meaningful statement.

Something I find very odd is that a distinguished philosopher of religion and epistemic logician, Alvin Plantinga, implies that this and/or logical trick means that the empirical meaning criterion cannot be used to challenge the meaningfulness of the statement "God exists." That is OK for logical games, but common-sensically—and scientifically—no one would accept the claim that a statement (such as "God exists") that can be neither proved nor disproved by ordinary experience is meaningful just because when it is linked by "and/or" with a statement such as "Grass is green" that can be proved to be true by ordinary experience, then the combined statement "'God exists' and/or 'Grass is green'" is meaningful. Yes, according to a rule of logic, it is. In the ordinary world, that rule does not apply.

Plantinga also asserts that God cannot do anything that is contradictory. In his *God and Other Minds*, he says:

> No one, presumably, expects an omnipotent being to be capable of performing such logically impossible actions as creating a square circle. (p. 169)

But that God can do *anything*, even logically impossible things, is a commonplace in Christian thought, as I show above. Descartes, for example, is a major proponent of this view. In a letter to Arnauld of 29 July 1648, Descartes says:

> I would not dare to say that God cannot make a mountain without a valley, or that 1 and 2 are not 3. I merely say that

God has given me such a mind that . . . such things involve a contradiction in my conception.

Consider again the conclusion that Descartes draws from God's possession of unlimited will. Because God can do *anything*, he can make contradictions such as 2 + 3 = 4 be true, really true. Given God's infinite power, there is no point in trying to figure out or in worrying about the contradictory demands God makes of human beings concerning what human beings can or cannot do to attain salvation. Pascal concurs with this view of the infinite power of God's will in a letter of 1656 to Charlotte Roannez, in which he says that "the reason why sins are sins is only that they are contrary to the will of God." From this, Pascal means Charlotte to be solaced by the fact that God could just as well have decreed that the thoughts she is worried about are not sinful.

In *Where the Conflict Really Lies*, Plantinga certainly avoids a lot of objections to the concept of God by saying that God cannot do anything contradictory, but he avoids these objections only by ignoring the implications of what it means to be omnipotent. Both Augustine and Descartes understood that if God creates everything, He also creates the rules. And if God is omnipotent, He can also break the rules.

Plantinga is a prolific defender of the existence of God, and a major opponent of in the so-called New Atheists (Dawkins, Dennett, Harris, Hitchens). In particular, he argues that theism is compatible with science and the theory of evolution, but not with materialism. In *Where the Conflict Really Lies: Science, Religion, and Naturalism*, Plantinga argues that in fact, God's guidance is the best explanation for some puzzling aspects of our world. He points out that

> several of the basic physical constants—the velocity of light, the strength of the gravitational force, and of the strong and weak nuclear forces—must fall within very narrow limits if intelligent life of our kind is to develop. (p. 194)

He argues that God's desire to make the Earth habitable by humans makes "such fine tuning is not at all surprising or improbable." (p. 199) He argues further that

Irreducibly complex structures and phenomena . . . can't have come to be . . . by gradual step-by-step Darwinian evolution. (p. 226)

He purports to show that

theistic religion gives us reason to expect our cognitive capacities to match the world in such a way as to make modern science possible. Naturalism [on the other hand] gives us no reason at all to expect this sort of match. (p. 303)

And he states that

The scientific theory of evolution just as such is entirely compatible with the thought that God has guided and orchestrated the course of evolution, planned and directed it, in such a way as to achieve the ends he intends. (p. 303)

The amazing thing is that Plantinga expects his readers to accept his totally undefended and unexplained premise that it makes sense that an all-powerful, self-caused God exists outside space and time, and that this God has created the universe and everything in it. If a reader accepts this, then that reader has no need for all of Plantinga's arguments and explanations, and if a reader does not accept this, then Plantinga is preaching to the choir.

Conflict, with all of Plantinga's wise-cracks and amusing asides, must be aimed at believers, and not at atheists. This would explain the fact that he passes over the problems raised by the premise of an all-powerful God Who creates everything: for example, Calvin's view about Predestination, that God chose who is to be saved and who damned the moment he created the universe, long before any humans existed.

I now give an extended quotation to show that Plantinga ignores any possibility that the premise of a God that creates everything, including Himself, might raise problems:

we don't think [a loving] God would choose or approve of genocide, hatred, and a whole list of ills our sorry race is heir to [but] God permits them because he has good reason—one that we may not be able to discern. . . . Here is one . . . God, the almighty first being of the universe and the creator of everything else, was willing to undergo enormous suffering in order to redeem creatures who had turned their backs on him. He created human beings; they rebelled against him and constantly go contrary to his will. Instead of treating them as some Oriental monarch would, he sent his Son, the Word, and the second person of the Trinity into the world. And the Word became flesh and dwelt among us. He was subjected to ridicule, rejection, and finally the cruel and humiliating death of the cross. . . . . All if this to enable human beings to be reconciled to God, and to achieve eternal life. This overwhelming display of love and mercy is not merely the greatest story ever told, it is the greatest story that *could be* told. No other great-making property of a world could match this one. (pp. 58–59)

This passage has all the elements of an "in your face" blast, not just at atheists, but also at agnostics, for whom the presence of evil at an overkill level—e.g., genocide—seems beyond theistic apologetics.

I have already remarked that the anthropologist Pascal Boyer argues that belief in the existence of supernatural powers such as gods and spirits has had survival value for the human species over the millennia. Certainly such beliefs have been a source of power for medicine men, witch doctors, priests, and priestesses throughout the ages. These charismatic men and women do have power over other human beings, whether or not they themselves believe in any supernatural source of their power. But probably most of these sorcerers really do believe that they have extraordinary powers, even if they also engage in a few tricks just to gain credence among ordinary people.

Where do these beliefs in the supernatural come from? Are we born with the belief in a supernatural God as Descartes believed? Boyer does not argue that belief in the supernatural is innate or that it is genetic. He just finds that all known human societies have such beliefs, and infers that therefore it must have survival value.

One proposed source of belief in the supernatural is that throughout much of the existence of the species, humans did not have natural or scientific explanations of the behavior of things. Everything seemed to have an inner power or spirit, and desires and powers to act of their own, just the way human beings do. Aristotle systematized this philosophy by saying that things have forms that have desires (stones desire to go to the center of the earth) and the power to attempt to fulfill those desires (just drop a stone and see). This theory is known as animism or spiritualism. Everything is like an animal that has a spirit with desires and the power to act to fulfill those desires. People in all human societies—including our own—have had beliefs in such animism.

Stories about these spirits—fairies, elves, trolls, witches, ghosts, gods and goddesses—have been told around campfires since the beginning of human time.

Why do little children make up notions of imaginary companions who are invisible and inaudible to everyone else? These imaginary companions provide comfort and companionship, as is the case in the play and movie *Harvey*, a tale of an adult (Jimmy Stewart in the movie) who was always accompanied by a six-foot-tall white rabbit that is invisible to everyone but him.

But can fears, fantasies, ignorance, and the imagination of storytellers be the ultimate source of the Christian belief that Jesus Christ (or God) is their continual companion? Certainly if someone insisted that he was always accompanied by a six-foot-tall white rabbit that only he could see, we would be suspicious of his claim. But people who have a spiritual, invisible, inaudible (to other people) companion in Jesus are seldom sent off to the loony bin.

On the other hand, most of us—even those with devout religious beliefs—are wary of people who strongly insist that Jesus or God speaks to them. It is distinctly worrisome when these people claim that these visitations have endowed them with the absolute Truth about how all human beings should believe and behave. Again I think of Reverend Jones, who precipitated mass suicide. How do you distinguish the saints from the crazies?

Putting the obvious loonies aside—but how does one tell?— the problems that arise when different sects of the same religion contradict one another about the Truth, as do Protestant and Catholic Christians, and Sunni and Shiite Muslims, cast doubt on the claims of each and all of them that their sect has access to the absolute Truth.

One way out of this impasse is just to admit, as scientists do and true believers do not, that humans have no access to any absolute Truth. This is a major difference between science and religion that Stephen Jay Gould does not grasp. There can be no congenial and open discussion between scientific and religious leaders in which each side respects the beliefs of the other, because the believers know the Truth and the scientists do not. The scientists are willing to compromise because they hold that all their theories are probable and none of them are absolutely true. Believers are not going to compromise with scientists because for believers to say that they do not have the absolute Truth would be the same as saying that they do not believe. The only way to gain Heaven is to believe absolutely that your God is the True God.

This is why there is an impasse between the Christian and Muslim faiths. I mention above that there were vicious religious wars between Protestant and Catholic Christians in the seventeenth century, even though they all believed that Jesus is the Son of God. The difference between Catholics and Protestants does not begin to be as extreme as the difference between Christians who believe that Jesus is the Son of God and their Savior, and Muslims who do not.

Many people know that Christmas and Easter come on the dates of pre-Christian religious ceremonies, and that Christianity is a survivor of a number of pre-Christian mystery religions. I am perfectly willing to accept the view that these facts do not stand as arguments against the truth of Christianity, as well as to accept the conclusion that belief in supernatural powers enhances human survival. The prehistoric origins of religion and the historic origins of Christianity could be as anthropologists and Bible scholars say, but none of this would be seen by believers as contradicting the Bible story of God and the divinity of Jesus Christ. I recognize this. I also understand the psychological value for many people of belief in God and religion, specifically Christianity. What I do not have are any religious feelings or beliefs of my own.

Why is this? Why am I bereft of religious sentiment and belief? As I have said, a lot of people who are a lot more intelligent than I am believe in God—and a lot more who are less intelligent than I am also believe in God. So intelligence is not definitive in belief.

In this investigation of the concept of God and belief in God, I have to face the fact that for many people, reason has nothing to do with their belief. Reason is inadequate to prove the existence of God to people like me, and reason is not a factor that leads to or supports the belief in God of believers. Once again, there seem to be two kinds of people in the world: Those who think that knowledge is based on reason and empirical experience, and those who think there is irrational, supernatural knowledge. The believers are enraptured, and the skeptics do not know what they are talking about.

Not all believers dismiss reason as a ground for belief in God. Remember that Alvin Plantinga—who is a Calvinist—denies the Augustinian interpretation of the power of the omnipotent God because it leads to logical contradictions. Numbers of believers (usually philosophers) do not want to give up the claim that empirical experience provides proof for God's existence. Blaise Pascal, for example, had an extremely intense ecstatic experience. He recorded the experience as follows:

The year of grace 1654
Monday the 23 November, feast of Saint Clement,
Pope and Martyr, and others in the Martyrology,
Eve of Saint Chrysogonus, Martyr and others.
From half past ten in the evening to half past midnight.
FIRE
"God of Abraham, God of Isaac, God of Jacob," [Ex.III.6.]
not of philosophers and scholars.
Certainty, certainty, heartfelt, joy, peace.
God of Jesus Christ.
God of Jesus Christ.
My God and your God. [John xx.17]
"Thy God shall be my God." [Ruth I.16]
The world forgotten, and everything except God.
He is to be found only by the ways taught in the Gospel.
Greatness of the human soul.
"O righteous Father, the world had not known thee,
but I have known Thee." [John xvii.23]
Joy, joy, joy, tears of joy.

I have cut myself off from Him.
They have forsaken me, the fountain of living waters. [Jer.II.13]
"My God wilt Thou forsake me?" [cf. Matt.xxvii.46]
Let me not be cut off from Him forever!
"And this is life eternal, that they might know thee,
the only true God, and Jesus Christ whom thou hast sent."
[John xvii.3]
Jesus Christ.
Jesus Christ.
I have cut myself off from Him, shunned him, denied
Him, crucified Him.
Let me never be cut off from Him!
He can be found only by the ways taught in the Gospels.
Sweet and total renunciation.
Total submission to Jesus Christ and my director.
Everlasting joy in return for one day's effort on earth.
I will not forget thy word. [Ps. cxix.16] Amen.

Pascal wrote this down on a piece of paper and kept it pinned inside his shirt for the rest of his life. I give it in full because it is one of the most revered and quoted description of an ecstatic religious experience in the modern Christian tradition, but also to comment on it.

Pascal was in a state of high religious tension on that day celebratory of many martyrs. He was hoping for, expecting some sort of sign to soothe and calm his intense worry about whether or not he was among God's elect who were predestined to be saved. This visitation assured him, but not completely, as shown by his last words on his deathbed that I have quoted above: "May God never abandon me!" which is foreshadowed in three lines from his report:

"My God wilt Thou forsake me?" [Jesus on the Cross]
Let me not be cut off from Him forever.
Let me never be cut off from Him.

Pascal thinks he has this assurance in his evocation of certainty and joy:

Certainty, certainty, heartfelt, joy, peace.
Joy, joy, joy, tears of joy.

Then there is a specific statement that the only source of knowledge about how to be saved is the Bible:

He can be found only by the ways taught in the Gospels.

And that one is to submit totally to Jesus and to the priest one has chosen to be one's director of conscience:

Total and sweet renunciation.
Total submission to Jesus Christ and my director.

This is the testimony of a devout Christian. It is in contrast to his older contemporary, René Descartes, who simply professed belief and then spent his time on earth not agonizing about that belief, but on investigations of the natural world that have led to his being called the Father of Modern Philosophy and Science. Pascal sought certainty in religion. Descartes is known for asserting that we cannot attain certainty in science, which is the primary principle that makes science open, non-dogmatic, and progressive—traits opposed to the certainty, dogmatism, and conservatism of organized religions such as Christianity.

Both Pascal and Descartes contributed enormously to the development of the modern world. But Pascal is by far more read and studied—and revered—today than Descartes.

You have perhaps noticed that the focus of this chapter has shifted 180 degrees. I started out wondering why anyone would believe in God. The focus has shifted to the question of why there are people like me who are either agnostic or do not believe in God. I cannot understand why anyone would believe in God, but apparently most people cannot understand why anyone would not believe in God. Or at least that is the case among Americans, predominantly Christians. Various studies have shown that up to 95 percent of Americans profess belief in God, and as many as 50 percent of them say they have had a religious experience.

I remark above that Jesse M. Bering states that the most current scientific explanation for such overwhelming belief that "a psychological susceptibility to belief in God is the result of adaptive design" (p. 143). Pascal Boyer explains that this design—"feature" is a better word, because "design" suggests there was a designer, which is not the case in evolutionary processes—is the result of the fact that belief in God contributes to the survival of the species. The reason why humans believe in supernatural beings and powers, according to this theory, is that the notion that we are constantly being watched by invisible beings with supernatural powers helps keep us honest, and thus contributes to the cohesion of society. Thus such famous atheists as Thomas Hobbes in the seventeenth and Karl Marx in the nineteenth century propose that state religions are necessary for controlling the masses. This led to the conspiracy theory that religion is imposed as the opiate of the people—so the lower classes will work in misery for a pittance with the promise of just rewards after death in Heaven, and thus capitalist property owners can get rich.

The view that religion is an inherent part of human nature seems confirmed by numerous failed attempts to wipe it out.

It appears that people like me who have no religious sentiments and have never had a religious experience are in the minority.

What is such a mystical religious experience like? It is being in a state of heightened awareness. It is a feeling of great exhilaration, of oneness with the universe or the scene at hand. This is common among climbers, explorers, participants in extreme sports. It seems to me now that I even had it occasionally while playing basketball in high school. But is that the same as what the mystics feel? From their descriptions, it seems so to me. But I have never had a feeling of contact with a higher power.

Some mystics have out-of-body experiences, the feeling that one is out of one's body and looking down on it. Probably almost everyone has had that feeling in dreams. Some mystics say that their experience is indescribable. But then they describe it as oceanic, one with the whole, great tranquility and peace, and so on. But if they cannot describe it at all, then is it really an experience?

Some say that it is like having a powerful orgasm that envelops your whole being. There is that famous sculpture by Gian Lorenzo Bernini, "The Ecstasy of Saint Teresa," who, as many critics have pointed out, looks as though she is in a state of sexual climax.

You know what? I am in over my head here. There are thousands of books by mystics and about mysticism. Check some of them out if you want. My claim is that ecstatic mystical experience proves nothing. Mystical experience proves nothing because there is no independent way of determining that the mystic is in contact with God, or even that an experience is mystical. How are experiences caused by drugs, fasting, meditation, determined to be mystical—and not just trips? The only evidence that such experiences are mystical encounters with the supernatural is the word of the mystics themselves. Beyond the fact that there is no way to check the mystic's claims, the results of trust in mystics are about the same as that for mediums and mind readers.

Yes, I am a skeptic. But, as Pascal says, these are important matters. Pascal says that if God exists, you do not want to be left behind. No, but on the other hand, neither do you want to be taken in by nonsense.

If you are going to commit yourself to belief in God—specifically here the Christian God—which belief implies many commitments you should make in the conduct of your life—worship of a God Who is ineffable, adherence to doctrines that are unintelligible, sacrifices of pleasures that appear harmless, acceptance of evils as the will of God, consignment to Hell of everyone but true Christian believers, and personal and intellectual humility before other human beings who are above you in the religious hierarchy (priests, cardinals, the pope, protestant ministers and bishops)—if you are going to commit yourself to belief in this Christian God, you would like to have some assurance that there is such a God. But if one must have assurance, one is not a true believer.

William James fastened onto the fact that there is no way to test in experience whether or not God exists. Empirical testing, which is the controlling method for determining truth and reality in natural science, is inapplicable to the question of God's existence. Whatever is the case in the world, it is compatible both with God's existence and God's non-existence. James said that because of this, you can believe or disbelieve in God as you wish. But believe in what? If there is nothing in the world that indicates whether or not God exists, if the world would be the same whether or not God exists, then at the very least God is not needed as creator of the world.

Some believers do try to provide empirical evidence (such as mystical experiences) for God's existence. One such is William Alston, a prominent analytic philosopher who is also a devout Christian. Like Plantinga, Alston is concerned to make belief in Christianity compatible with the principles and findings of reason, logic, and the confirmation principles of natural science. He does not go so far as to claim to have had mystical experiences, but he does propose that there are empirical experiences that count as evidence for God's existence. Here is his major attempt along these lines:

> I take as my starting point the conviction that somehow what goes on in the experience of leading the Christian life provides some ground for Christian belief, makes some contribution to the rationality of Christian belief. We sometimes feel in the presence of God; we get glimpses, at least, of God's will for us; we feel the Holy Spirit at work in our lives, guiding us, strengthening us, enabling us to love other people in a new way; we hear God speaking to us in the Bible, in preaching, or in the words and actions of our fellow Christians. Because of all this we are more justified in our Christian beliefs than we would have been otherwise. I am not suggesting that this is the whole ground or that it can do the whole job. (p. 103)

> The Christian beliefs under consideration say that God will manifest Himself in certain ways in our . . . experience. . . . This provides empirical confirmation for the beliefs . . . in question. (p. 105)

The ways God manifests himself, according to Alston, are in the feelings he describes above. I have no doubt that Alston has those feelings, and that they comfort him and guide him in his life. But it is amazing to see an analytic philosopher such as Alston proposing these feelings even as "some" evidence that justifies his belief in God. These feelings obviously constitute experience that explains his belief in God, but they are not evidence that God exists.

All kinds of people have all kinds of feelings. I am sure there are people who have the feeling that they are going to win the lottery today. The pot is $365 million, the largest so far in the United States. Sure, I bought a ticket. I know about Pascal's wager.

Now after reading this far, what do you think of my chances of winning the lottery as compared with Pascal's chances of going to Heaven? Fellow philosophers chastise me for buying lottery tickets. The chances of winning are infinitesimal, they say. Yes, I say, there are two ways of looking at it. Either your chance is one out of trillions, or it is fifty/fifty—you either win or you lose. Pascal makes the same shift with his wager. The chance of God's existing so far as empirical evidence goes is, if not zero, at least in the zillions. But Pascal says that God either exists or he does not, fifty/fifty, so you had better believe in God, and do all the proper Christian things, just in case. That would be like me buying a lottery ticket on the grounds that the chances of my winning are fifty/fifty. I'll either win or lose.

The analogy seems obvious, but let me pound it into the ground. I would be in deep trouble if I put all my savings into lottery tickets and did not win. (Later: Eight garbage collectors from Michigan won the pot.) But what if I believed in God and God did not exist? Pascal said I would have lost nothing. But that is not true. If I changed my life to be a devout Christian, I would lose a lot of satisfactions that I now enjoy. Many of these satisfactions appear totally harmless to me (and to others), but are forbidden by Christian beliefs. I would also lose a lot of time spent on Church matters that I now spend doing other things I enjoy (and find harmless).

Of course you could say that I would be dead, and if there were no God or afterlife, it would not matter to me, because I would not be.

Right.

Alston remarks that

> it is often contended that one is making a genuine factual claim . . . only if it is in principle possible to *disconfirm* what one is saying [and] it is clear that our examples are not decisively disconfirmable by experience. . . there can be no negative instances; whatever happens, you cannot take it as evidence that [God does not exist]. (pp. 105–106)

It is embarrassing to see Alston (like Plantinga) threshing about trying to show that it is reasonable to believe that God exists. He knows he cannot show that, so he says that "Reasoning is but one among many modes of belief formation" (p. 172). That is quite true.

We form beliefs for all sorts of reasons, one being wishful thinking. But beliefs formed by reasoning are the only ones that can be tested. Or more to the point, beliefs formed by reasoning are the only ones that can be trusted.

So are there any grounds for religious beliefs other than one's own convictions and feelings? Alston concludes by saying that

> we must look outside our own [inadequate] experience to the tiny minority that qualify as masters of the spiritual life, both for some intimation of what mastery of this practice is like and for an answer to the question of whether this enterprise proves itself by its fruits . . . [we must look to] the likes of Mother Teresa of Calcutta as to what it is to be more than babes in the experience of God, and as to what it is to respond to this experience in the ways it indicates. (p. 182)

Mother Teresa, I understand, was a hard woman. She even said that during the last fifty or so years of her life she had lost her faith. But she still behaved like a saint. The Catholic hierarchy seems particularly fond of such cases, and probably will make her a saint. As for Alston, in the end (actually, from the beginning) he is preaching to the choir. He is intelligent enough to know this.

Nicholas Wolterstorff in the same volume asks "Can Belief in God be Rational If It Has No Foundations?" Like Alston, he argues not for belief, but from belief. He says that

> some of our dispositions are signs of our fallenness, not part of our pristine nature, so that they are not reliable. The dispositions of which Marx and Freud made so much of are examples. . . . May it not also be that sometimes the nonrationality of one's conviction that God exists is a trial, to be endured? (p. 164)

I have not picked Plantinga, Alston, and Wolterstorff to discuss because they are easy to criticize. I have picked them because they are highly skilled analytic philosophers who argue for the existence of the Christian God. But I suspect that their writings on religion (and similar such writings by other believers) are part of the reason many scientists ignore or make fun of professional philosophers.

What should be said here is that Alvin Plantinga, William Alston, Nicolas Wolterstorff, and the philosopher who said that in God's eyes the Holocaust is good all have been presidents of the American Philosophical Association.

And so, opposed to John Toland, Christianity is mysterious. God is mysterious.

And it happens that a number of contemporary philosophers led by Colin McGinn are known as *mysterians*. Mental consciousness, they say, is a mysterious phenomenon that can never be explained, and certainly not in terms of physical science. Unlike most neurophysiologists and philosophers of mind today, mysterians do not believe that the mind is the brain. Mysterians claim that they are not dualists, but agree that the mental and the physical appear to be two different, totally incompatible things that somehow are linked as one. But how the mind and the body are related, they assert (just as Descartes did), will forever remain an eternal mystery.

Human beings always have loved a mystery. The success of the mystery religions based on the Old Testament, the New Testament, and the Koran testify to this. Mind-body dualism gives rise to the great mystery of how these two incompatible things can interact. The answer is that they cannot. So belief in mind-body interaction must—just like belief in God—be based on faith. What are the grounds for this mind-body interaction? They are pretty much the same grounds proposed by those who believe in the existence of God because God is inscrutable, ineffable, and totally beyond human comprehension. They believe in God *because* God is a great mystery beyond human comprehension. So, also, according to the Mysterians, is the interaction between mind and body a great mystery beyond human comprehension. Just as the believers begin with the absolute assurance that God exists, and then say that what God is, is a mystery, so do the Mysterians begin with the absolute assurance that mind and body are compatible, and then say that their interaction is a mystery beyond human comprehension.

In contrast to the Mysterians who believe (despite their claim not to) in a dualism of mind and body, monistic philosophers and most neuroscientists believe that there is only one sort of stuff in the universe out of which everything is made. Mental and physical phenomena are certainly very different, but, say the anti-Mysterians (that is, almost all scientists), no matter how difficult it is to explain how conscious mental phenomena can arise out of a physical world, scientists will eventually work out this explanation. But until such an explanation is confirmed, Mysterians, like Christians, can maintain the belief that the soul will survive the death of the body.

Pascal said that the *only* thing a human being should be concerned with is the salvation of one's soul. It seems possible that at bottom Mysterians hope that as long as the mind has not been shown to be a function of the material brain, as long as it has not been demonstrated that the brain is the mind, then it will still be possible that humans might have immortal souls.

Let's regroup.

The basic challenge to disbelief in supernatural religion is an attack on reason itself. In particular, believers reject the principle of non-contradiction, the principle that any contradictory concept or statement is meaningless. Thus, it is *stated* (not argued) that the self-contradictory concept of God is meaningful. Never mind that logically speaking, we do not know what we are talking about when we talk about God, God still exists. Furthermore, the empirical meaning criterion is rejected, the commonsense foundation of scientific knowledge, the principle that if there is no conceivable way in experience to decide whether a proposition is true or false, then that proposition is meaningless.

In the Bible, and in Church tradition, one is instructed to take the conclusion that God exists on faith. Do not try to understand it. Be ye as little children. Accept the wisdom of the Pope and the Fathers of the Church. After all, a good rule when facing a really difficult question, is to accept the views of exceptionally intelligent people. One problem here is figuring out who to trust, and another is that even the geniuses disagree.

But all believers agree that God exists.

Pascal and the eighteenth-century skeptic Voltaire, for example, are among the most intelligent people who ever lived. Pascal says the heart has reasons reason does not know, and so one can believe that God exists, even if one does not understand what "God" means.

Voltaire says such "belief" is vacuous, superstitious nonsense. Pascal chooses the side of faith and Voltaire chooses the side of reason. You might think the issue here is whether one should follow faith or reason.

But no, the foundational question is, *can* one choose the side of Pascal? *Can* one choose the side of unreason, of irrationality? If having a position depends on making sense of the doctrines of the side of unreason—either empirical or logical sense—then the answer is no. But Pascal would say that to depend on making sense is explicitly to choose the side of reason against the side of faith, rational vs. irrational, natural vs. supernatural. If you insist that you have to *understand* the choice of faith, then you have chosen the side of reason. But on the other hand, if you agree that you can chose the side of faith without understanding it, then you have chosen the side of irrational unreason.

You cannot make an open, unprejudiced, even choice between faith and reason. Whichever one you choose rules out not just the possibility of your choosing the other. It also rules out the meaningfulness of your choosing the other. Chose reason, and faith is unintelligible. Chose faith, and reason is irrelevant.

The above comments depend on accepting the proposal that one *can* choose between faith and reason. But the choice may not be free. Pascal speaks for believers when he says that the heart has its reasons that reason knows not.

Pascal's remark about the reasons of the heart is famous, but it is no more than the statement that for some people "heartfelt" beliefs override reason. But philosophers such as Plantinga and Alston would like to keep belief in God within the realm of reason and commonsense knowledge of the world. Believers are just not going to get anywhere in attempts to convince people who reject irrationality to take Jesus as their Savior.

But perhaps there is another way.

In reasoning about mathematics and the world, we start with the assumed logical principle of non-contradiction and the empirical meaning criterion.

So in reasoning about God and religion, why not just begin with the unproved, foundational assumption that God exists?

OK, but then what happens?

The crucial difference between starting with the principles of non-contradiction and the empirical meaning criterion, as contrasted to starting with the existence of God, is that our experience of the world confirms that objects such as square circles do not exist, and that things in the world do add up mathematically. This principle of non-contradiction and the empirical meaning criterion are foundations of our highly successful modern science. But as I have often remarked in this chapter, nothing that happens in this world proves or disproves that God exists. Obviously—as Saint Thomas has done—one can postulate the existence of God and go on from there to build a grand cathedral of belief, but it has no substance or foundation in the world we live in. Again, nothing that happens in the world proves or disproves the existence of God. Whether or not God exists seems to make no difference to the world.

Except psychologically. Belief in the existence of God gives lots of people the comfort and courage to go on in a world that looks more and more cruel and meaningless as the centuries march on. Belief in God supports such productive people as Jane Goodall. Of course a lot of the horror in human existence is imposed by believers on other people in the name of religion. A great tragedy of faith and belief is that believers in the Truth perpetuate evil on non-believers. This is done even by people who follow the Golden Rule: Do unto others as you would have them do unto you. This is not just a benign and pious religious admonition. It is a call to Crusade and Jihad. It justifies those who *know* that they believe in the True God in their persecution of unbelievers and those of other faiths. The Golden Rule can be used to support the bloody conversion of the unenlightened by those who *know* they know the Truth. You would surely want to be brought into the fold, even bloodily, by believers, if it truly were for your own good—for the salvation of your soul.

I am not just making debating points here. This travesty of the Golden Rule makes perfect sense in true, Augustinian Christianity. In Adam's sin, sinned we all. Human beings *cannot* not sin, not even in following the Golden Rule. Because of the Fall, we cannot freely do good, even if we want to. The only way we can do good is if we are determined to do so by the Grace of God. Only through the Grace of

God can we avoid behaving sinfully in all our actions. Here we have come full circle again to the foundational paradox of Christianity.

But God created Adam!

Chapter 2.
Free Will and the Mind-Body Problem

My father in his hospital bed looked at me and said, "It's all right." He took a few rasping breaths and then he died. He was eighty years old and might have lived to be a hundred, because, the doctor said, he had a heart like a water buffalo. His heart is why, emaciated as he was from several operations and being fed through tubes, it took him more than two weeks to starve himself to death. His problem was that a non-malignant tumor in his colon finally grew so large that it blocked the passage. This led to an emergency operation in a small-town Iowa clinic by a doctor who knew theoretically what to do but was no surgeon. The doctor was a big man, a former college football player, and when he came out of surgery he was exhausted and completely soaked with sweat. It had taken him four hours to get the tumor out and the colon sewn back together.

"I thought we had lost him several times," he said.

It was a patch job. Where the colon had been sewn together adhesions formed and closed it again. Two more operations followed, now by surgeons in Omaha. They left a hole in the colon and installed an external bag. All of this required long bouts of intravenous fluids and feeding through tubes down his throat. My father was game at first and told the Omaha surgeon to go ahead with an operation to remove the bag and sew the colon back together again. More adhesions formed and they had to cut the old man open yet again. His kidneys failed and he had to go on dialysis.

It had been eighteen months since the first operation. My father said, "This is no way to live," and he quit eating. He was back in the small-town Iowa clinic by then. When he told his regular doctor, an old friend, to take out the needles and tubes, there was no protest. If you are old and want to die with dignity and no nonsense about

68

prolonging a miserable life, go to a small-town clinic in the great Midwest. There you will be understood.

For years my father had told no one (although my mother suspected it) that he was having trouble with his bowels. The reason for his silence is that he was born and raised in the Missouri Ozarks. A hillbilly knows that if you seriously have to go to the doctor, you're dead. Sure, he had a Master's degree from the University of Iowa and had been a high school teacher, coach, and superintendent for nearly fifty years. But in his soul he was still down on the farm. He thought he had cancer. He did not. That tumor could have been snipped out years before with no problem whatsoever. Believe me, my brother and I went right out and had colonoscopies, and had a few non-malignant tumors removed.

Yes, the great Midwest. In another small Iowa town, my father-in-law also starved himself to death. I understand that this is quite common among old folks who are ready to die. He was eighty-five, and he did have cancer. "People sure are goddamned idiots to smoke," he said. The idiot he had in mind was himself. He had quit twenty years before, but he still got lung cancer. He was in pain and he knew how even more painful the radiation treatments and chemotherapy would be. The cancer would kill him in any case. So he said to Hell with it, and mostly quit eating. It took about a month for him to die. When he did, his wife, two daughters, two sons-in-law, his dog, the hospice nurse, and the family doctor were all present in the room with him. He muttered something none of us caught, and then he was gone.

Perhaps you have seen it yourself. One moment the person is there. The next moment he is not and you call the undertaker to come get the body. Whatever it was that lived and thought and talked through that body simply vanishes. The conscious person with its joys and troubles, memories, hopes and fears, is gone. The personality that expressed and experienced itself through that body is as though it had never been. Gone. Oddly enough, for most people who watch it happen, it is not even eerie. It just happens. The switch is turned off. Breathing stops, the heart quits beating. The machine shuts down. It is so abrupt, however, that it is not surprising that most people throughout history have thought that whatever was conscious in that body must still exist. The person cannot be entirely gone. Surely the soul survives. The care with which Neanderthals buried their dead shows that 50,000 years ago people thought there was an afterlife. In every human society there is the fear of ghosts, the spirits of the dead. The belief that something of our selves survives our death is universal among humankind.

I am a retired university philosophy professor. I have been studying and teaching one of the great philosophers of the human soul, René Descartes, for more than sixty years. René Descartes was the seventeenth-century philosopher who said, "I think, therefore I am." If you know you are thinking, you know you exist. For suppose you try to deny that you exist. Who is doing the denying? This leads to a great joke. A student comes in and says, "Tell me, professor, I've been worrying all night. Do I exist?" The professor sighs and says to the student, "So who wants to know?"

What goes when the body dies? The person, we say, the self-conscious person who moved and expressed itself through that body. And the immediate question that arises is: Where does that person go? Well, where was it when the body was alive? It was in the living body. People used to think of it being in the heart. Today we say it is in the mind that occupies the brain. And what is it? Christian belief is that it is in the soul. What is lost when a person dies is the self that manifests itself in the mind or soul that occupies a living human body.

For Descartes, the mind and the soul are the same thing.

Minds or souls are created by God, Who unites them with human bodies. At death, human bodies disintegrate. But human souls, being immaterial, can survive the death of the body. Thus Descartes's philosophy satisfies Christian doctrine. But unless that soul is aware or conscious of itself, its survival would not be of much interest to you. Thus consciousness of self is essential to the soul.

Because consciousness of self is essential both to the mind and to the soul, philosophers since Descartes have often used the terms mind and soul interchangeably, and I follow that usage.

Descartes set up the mind-body problem that continues to bedevil philosophers to the present day. The problem derives from Descartes's notions of what mind and body consist of.

What is essential to being a mind is self-consciousness. This is because if you were not conscious of yourself thinking, then *you* would not be thinking. Your mind, then, is a thinking thing. This is in contrast to your body, which is not a thinking thing, but is a material thing. Descartes concluded that the mind is an unextended thinking thing, and the body is an unthinking extended thing.

The mind-body problem is to determine how a thinking, unextended immaterial mind and an unthinking extended material body can causally interact, as happens, for example, every time one's mind moves the human body it occupies by mentally deciding to do so, and whenever one's mind feels sensations when that body's sense organs are physically stimulated.

One material body moves another by pushing or bumping it. A law of classical physics is that there is no action at a distance. For one body to move another, the two bodies must come into contact. Now consider the fact that when we move about freely according to our desires and intentions, our minds cause our bodies to move. This is amazing. How can immaterial minds bump into material bodies to make them move? They cannot.

Here is another way of seeing the problem. Consider that old question: How many angels can dance on the head of a pin? Of course it is a trick question with two opposite, equally good answers. You can say that an infinite number of angels can dance on the head of a pin because immaterial angels take up no space. So any number of angels can rock and roll on a pin's head. On the other hand, you can say not even one, not a single angel, can dance on the head of a pin because the dear little things have no feet. My students used to groan at that joke.

If soul and body cannot bump into one another, then souls cannot move bodies, nor bodies souls.

But body and soul do interact! We experience both bodily effects on our thinking minds, and mental effects on our bodies' behavior. How can this be? Descartes was asked this question by Princess Elisabeth (in a letter of 6 May 1643). Descartes's answer (of 28 June 1643) is quite brief. We know that mind and body interact because we experience it all the time. Such interaction seems impossible, but God can do anything, even if it seems to us contradictory. God can make a mountain without a valley. God can make mind and body interact. So quit worrying about it.

It is, however, so clearly obvious that immaterial minds and material bodies cannot really interact that the seventeenth-century Cartesian Nicholas Malebranche developed a metaphysical position called occasionalism. Because mind and matter cannot interact, Malebranche said, God himself causes our minds to have sensations and ideas every time other bodies interact with our sense organs. As for the mind's influence on the body, Malebranche said that on the occasion, for example, of my desiring to raise my arm, God raises my arm for me. It appears to us as though real mind-body interaction is taking place, but it is not. For every occasion of apparent causal interaction between mind and matter, God is the real and only causal force. Why God would want to set things up in this complicated, deceptive, and time-consuming (although of course God does not exist in time) way is something Malebranche never explained.

Even if we cannot explain how we do it, we certainly seem to be able to move our bodies. The problem is that according to our highly confirmed science of physics, the movements of all material things are caused only by the previous movements of other material things. In turn, movements of those material things are caused by preceding material movements that extend all the way back to the Big Bang. Or all the way back to the creation of the world by God (and there is no reason why God could not have done this with the Big Bang).

The behavior of all these material things is determined by the laws of physics (God's laws). So how can an immaterial mind overcome and alter the movements of a human body? A human body is, after all, just another material body whose movements are determined by the previous movements of other material bodies. Thus by all logic it is impossible for acts of mental free will to alter these deterministic material movements. In Descartes's terms, it is a contradiction to say that a material body can give rise to nonmaterial thoughts, or that a nonmaterial mind can move a material body. That is why Malebranche decided that God does it for us. Of course traditionally God, too, is immaterial. So if God moves bodies, His doing so is a miracle. (Miracles are defined as anything that is not determined by the laws of physics or nature. Of course everything God does is a miracle.)

In modern physics, some slack is introduced into the absolute determinism of classical physics. In absolute determinism, a given physical effect will follow a given physical cause 100 percent of the time. But many natural laws are statistical, but still deterministic. For example, only about five percent of people with untreated syphilis get paresis. What is determined in this case is not what will happen each time the cause occurs, but rather that for every one hundred occurrences of the cause, the effect will follow five times.

Besides statistical laws, there are elements of chance in the behavior of the sub-atomic particles that make up atoms. For example, there is no law of cause and effect such that one can predict even statistically the next position of an electron. But when one gets to the level of things composed of atoms—rocks, chairs, our own bodies—the random behavior of sub-atomic particles averages out to the deterministic behavior of the large bodies. For the common-sense bodies in the world we live in, the deterministic laws of physics hold without exception.

Given deterministic physics, the choices one makes, then, would seem to be extraneous and to have no causal influence on one's body's motions whatsoever; they are secondary, redundant, and unnecessary; they have no causal efficacy at all.

On this view, consciousness itself, and especially consciousness of making decisions to move one's body, is at most merely an awareness of one's bodily motions that are necessarily determined by their interactions with other bodies. One's sense of self-determination—the feeling that one's will is free and that one's free choices cause one's actions—would then be a deception that arises when the physical causes take effect.

There seems to be no solution to the problem of how immaterial mind and material body could actually interact as Descartes and almost everyone else think they do. So the eighteenth-century philosopher George Berkeley simply denied that matter exists. He was a complete mentalist. For him, all that exists are minds and their sensations and ideas. Our bodies are merely all the sensations that we have when we say we see and feel our bodies. There is no material body underlying and causing these sensations. God causes them. So we do not have to worry about the interaction of mind with matter.

This position is variously called idealism, mentalism, phenomenalism, and spiritualism. It satisfied a number of religious philosophers throughout the nineteenth century, but few philosophers hold it today. The reason is that for mentalists, there are no scientific explanations of how the world appears to us because all our ideas and sensations come directly to our minds from God. That is, we know what sensations follow other sensations, and we can make up theories about material bodies, but none of these bodies actually exists. What actually exists are just all those sensations God gives us. Most people find this mentalism theory to be totally unsatisfactory. The only reason one can give for how and why things are as they are is that God presents them that way. Thus on the mentalist view, we can never figure out how bodies interact according to natural laws. All we can do is discover what sensations God has ordained to follow one another.

Just a note here: Why should any Christian object to Berkeley's immaterialism? After all, Christians believe that God created everything. If God wanted to create an immaterial world that appears to consist of interacting material bodies, He could do it. In fact, under the name of Idealism this theory has been adopted by a number of prominent Christian philosophers, for example Josiah Royce at Harvard.

A more promising mentalist position is Aristotle's view that the causal powers of different kinds of souls (he calls them forms) provide the power for everything to be what it is and to do what it does. The formative soul of an acorn causes it to grow into an oak tree. The classic argument against this view was given by Molière in his play *The Imaginary Invalid*. When the doctor in the play is asked why opium puts people to sleep, he replies that it is because opium has a dormitive power. In plain words, opium puts you to sleep because it has the power to put you to sleep. You already knew that. Of course an acorn turns into an oak tree because it has the power to do so. The question is how. It does not help much to be told that something is and behaves the way it does because it is its nature to do so.

Aristotle's system is a formalization of the ancient doctrine of panpsychism. This is the view that everything has a spirit, or a soul, or a mind that controls it. The world is said to be teeming with these spirits, all of which are in bodies, and each of which contends with all the others to maintain its place in the world. They exist in a dog-eat-dog world, a world of war of all against all, which is how the seventeenth-century philosopher Thomas Hobbes described the human condition. But there are only—at last estimate—seven billion human beings. If everything has a spirit, just think of the immense struggle of zillions upon zillions of spirits competing to survive and prosper. The nineteenth-century German philosopher Arthur Schopenhauer argued that the universe itself is nothing but a primal, blind, unconscious force of will-to-be that manifests itself in the voracious, violent emergence of everything in the world.

This panpsychic view of the world as consisting of myriad spiritual beings has never led to any advancement of science or technology. This is because the only approaches to these spirits are to beg, threaten, praise, or pray, none of which is effective at all. Even supposing these spirits do exist, no one has ever found any evidence that we can contact or control them. Nevertheless, panpsychism has a strong pull on the human psyche. This is demonstrated every time you kick or swear at a chair you have stumbled over. Or when your grandfather is driving up a steep hill, he says to his vintage Buick, "Come on Bessie, you can make it." The fact is that no one has ever managed to get material things to do anything by talking to them unless those material things are living bodies with minds that can understand what you say and act on what you command. Even there the range is limited. A famous animal trainer—so I have heard—once said, "You can talk to a dog and eventually it will understand what you want it to do, and the dog will do it. But you can talk to a rabbit until you are blue in the face, and it will never understand a word you say."

But we don't move our bodies by talking to them. We move by exerting our mental power of will. Again, how is this possible?

The scientific evidence that the motions of all material bodies in the world, including our own bodies, are strictly determined is very strong. But let's suppose that we actually do have efficacious free will exhibited as the ability to control many of our bodies' movements.

How does the mind act on the body? We have been considering the standard answer that extends back at least to the ancient Egyptians. Each of us has a soul (mind) that has the simple brute power to move the human body it occupies. If this is just to say that the soul has the power to move the body because it has the power to move the body, then so be it. That is just the way it is, as anybody who got out of bed this morning knows. So let's look again at Aristotle's forms. He believed, and many animists, spiritualists, and panpsychists still believe, that everything has an active form—call it a soul—that has the power to seek what it desires and to avoid what it does not. According to Aristotle, all heavy bodies, for example, have an urge to move to the center of the earth. Therefore they push down. All the time. This explains why they feel heavy and why they fall when they are not restrained. Try it. Let go of a rock in mid-air. Notice that it rushes toward the center of the earth until it is stopped by the ground. See?

Descartes said that the notion that bodies have all these forms and powers is absurd. Aristotle's mistake was to think that because human beings have souls with the power to move their own bodies, then everything that moves (even if it is only a rock that falls to the ground) has such a soul. But according to Descartes, only human beings have souls. Even non-human animals that appear to behave freely and willfully, such as horses and dogs, are only soulless machines. They are merely material bodies being pushed around by other material bodies.

Descartes's Christian contemporaries were afraid that his view that everything in nature including human bodies is a machine would lead to complete materialism, to the view that even human beings are just material machines. They worried about this even though Descartes said all living human bodies are united with souls. Descartes was a mind-body dualist, that is, he believed there are two kinds of substances in the universe, mental minds and material bodies. But no Cartesian has ever been able to explain how the soul can interact with the body. This is one reason why many philosophers today are monistic materialists who believe that there is only one kind of substance in the universe, matter. But the main reason why they believe that everything that exists is material, including minds and feelings and thoughts, is because materialism leads to comprehensible explanations of how things in the physical universe work—mechanistically in Descartes's day—and mentalism does not. Materialism has led to vast advances in science and technology, and mentalism has not.

The mind or soul or spirit most people believe in today has not changed at least since the seventeenth century. It is still conceived of as an active, immaterial, thinking substance that is the diametric opposite of matter. But matter today is not thought of as Descartes's inert, extended, passive substance. Scientists today agree that bodies have four forces: gravitational, electromagnetic, and weak and strong nuclear forces. As opposed to classical physics, such forces allow bodies to act on one another at a distance. They do not have to bump into one another. But most scientists do not believe that there are any mental forces. There just is no confirmed evidence for mental forces, as I discuss below.

The crucial point here is that matter as conceived of today is just as opposite to the mental as is Cartesian extended matter. No one yet has shown how minds conceived of as immaterial mental entities have the force or power to move this matter. Finally, none of the forces of matter can conceivably act on an immaterial soul.

Certainly anyone who believes that the soul survives the death of the body does not believe that the soul is a material body. Bodies disintegrate. Most emphatically, immortalists do not believe that the immaterial soul is dependent for its existence on the body. It can exist entirely on its own. The gulf between body and soul continues in the twenty-first century to be absolute.

Chapter 3.

The Soul

Materialists believe that only one kind of substance exists, matter. They avoid the mind-body problem by denying that the mind is a mental substance. They say that the mind is merely the operating material brain. If the mind is the brain, then everything that has been traditionally designated as mental is in fact material. Most scientists are materialists even though two major problems concerning the contradictory natures of the mental and the material remain. The first problem is how a material body could have or feel a sensation. For example, if you stick yourself in the arm with a pin, neither the pin nor your arm feels pain, but you do. The feeling is not a property of either the pin or the wound, but neither does it seem to be a property of your brain. The feeling is mental, not material.

The other problem derives from the fact that in themselves, all ideas and many sensations are about things other than themselves, but material things in themselves are not about anything. Thus ideas and many sensations are representational. It is in their very nature to picture, describe, be about, or point to things. But material things as such do not point to or represent other things. We can designate material things to be signs of or to represent other things, of course, but no material thing, just as a material thing, is about anything else.

But if the mind and everything mental is actually material as most scientists believe today, then sensory feelings and aboutness must also be material. But how can a *material* sensation have feelings and be about things?

Consider sensations: the taste of butterscotch *as tasted*, the odor of lilacs *as smelled*, the sound of music *as heard*, the roughness of tree bark *as felt*, and the red color of a rose *as seen*. These sensory experiences appear to be entirely mental. They have an *as felt, as experienced, as sensed* nature. Material things do not have odors *as smelled*, visual images *as seen*, and so on. Material things have size, shape, and position. They are in motion or at rest. They attract or repel other bodies. They respond to forces of gravity and electromagnetism, and to strong and weak nuclear forces. They combine and break apart. But they do not feel anything. They do not point to anything. Tickles and itches. Moods, passions, obsessions, desires, aversions, hopes, and fears. None of these can be described in material terms.

Moreover, the sensations you feel are yours alone. No one can feel them but you. Only you can have your sensations. If someone else had them, they would be that person's sensations, not yours. Sensations are not shared. Sensations are private. Our thoughts, imaginations, and ideas also are private. No one but you can feel *your* pain. No one but you can see the visual images you see or imagine. All your thoughts and sensations are thus subjective in the sense that they belong to only one subject—you.

On the other hand, material bodies are public. You and I can sit on the same bench. We can look at the same tree in the same meadow. Or we do experiments on the same chemicals in the same laboratory using the same equipment. All of those bodies are public. Unlike sensations and ideas, material things do not belong exclusively to anyone. In fact, in their essential nature, they do not belong to anyone at all. They just are.

This notion of private mental sensations and public material bodies leads to the greatest difference between mental and material things. Sensations and ideas exist only when they are felt or thought. They are discontinuous. Bodies exist whether or not anyone thinks about them, observes them, or manipulates them. A pain has to be felt or imagined by someone to exist. If a pain or an idea is to exist, you have to be able to answer the question: Who is having it? But the material world of bodies exists whether or not anyone is thinking of it or doing anything to it. Even if there were no minds, the material world would still exist.

The mental and the material are thus so different from one another that it seems quite impossible that the mind could be the brain. Nevertheless, there is a great deal of neurophysiological evidence that suggests that this is the case.

Now consider the fact that our sensations and ideas are about other things in the world. The technical term for this is that they have intentionality. They intend or point to other objects. This aboutness is part of their intrinsic nature, part of what makes them sensations and ideas.

But no material things are essentially about other things. It is just not in the nature of any material thing to be about, point to, or mean anything. No material body is intentional. But here is a crucial fact that sometimes confuses people about this matter. We can *use* or *take* any material thing at all to be about, point to, or mean anything we want it to. For example, we can put a lighted lantern in the window to indicate that the coast is clear. But even when a material thing is about something, its aboutness is not part of its nature. The aboutness of material things is something we impose on them. A material thing can be about something only when we take it to be about that thing. We make it into a symbol of a thing. We can use absolutely anything to mean anything at all.

Two kinds of material things that everyone uses all the time to mean things are spoken noises and written marks on paper (or a computer screen). Speech and writing convey meanings because we intend them to mean something. Mere noises and marks on paper mean nothing. There would be no meanings in the world if there were no symbol-using beings like us who assign meanings to things or take things to have meanings.

The mind-brain problem is as much an unsolved conundrum today as it was in the seventeenth century. As I remark above, the insolubility of the problem of how an immaterial mind or soul and a material body can interact led George Berkeley to argue that there is no body, only the soul. Equally, it is why Thomas Hobbes argued that there is no soul, only body. Most philosophers of mind and neuroscientists today are materialists like Hobbes. They argue that the brain does everything the mind or soul is supposed to do. Thus when the body dies and the brain rots, the soul vanishes.

Oh! But would that I did have an immortal soul, that I could be self-conscious and aware of all that goes on about me from here to eternity. The pleasures of life are inexhaustible. I do get tired, but then sweet sleep revives me for the dawn of yet another day. But would that after each night's rest a new day dawned for me forever. Oh that my day were as long as the coming night! For I love life. I want to do so many things. Even in old age I have a dozen lifetimes planned. Yet I will die. My body is wearing out and one day it will give up the ghost. But am I not that ghost? The self of which I am conscious, the personal me that I am, will that spark of life not survive?

Enough of that. But you see what I mean.

To survive after the death of your body, you as a bodiless soul or mind must be able to be or do at least the following things:

First, your soul must be self-conscious. Self-consciousness is what makes you your own person. First and foremost, you must remain the same person after death that you were before death.

Second, your disembodied soul must be able to have all the sensations you now have, of taste, smell, hearing, touch, and sight, and moods, emotions, and passions. Without these, you would not be yourself. If there is a Heaven and Hell, our disembodied souls must be able to feel pleasure and pain to be rewarded or punished.

Third, your bodiless soul must be able to reason and think, remember and imagine. You must be able to use your senses, reason, memory, and imagination to know what is going on, to act in the present, and to plan for the future.

Fourth and finally, you must be able to know where you are and be able to move from place to place. In other words, if we move on to another world, we want to inhabit that world as we do this one. Otherwise our primary concern—to be united with our loved ones, to see them, to embrace them, to talk to them—would not be possible.

Plato believed that every soul has always existed and always will. When the body a soul occupies dies, that soul moves on to another living body. In this transmigration, however, no soul ever remembers its previous experiences in earlier bodies. Each time a soul inhabits a new body, it is as though that soul were newly created for the first time. Thus there is no persisting person, no self that remains the same as a soul moves from one body to the next. So if Plato's notion of the soul were correct, it would be a blow to people who seek immortality, for on his view, the persons we are now do not survive the deaths of our bodies.

There may be one soul for many successive bodies, but there is only one self-conscious person for each body. The person or conscious personality—which is the notion of the mind or soul that interests us—is strictly mortal.

A very popular notion is that souls that transmigrate from one body to the next *do* remember their previous lives. Shirley McLaine is a strong believer in this view. So is her comic strip double, Boopsie, in *Doonsbury*. Actually, it is not clear that Boopsie's soul once was Hunk-Rah. It may be that a channel is opened between her body and the soul of Hunk-Rah, who takes over her body now and then to express himself. This would be a form of possession, which I discuss below.

Let's get back to transmigration. It does sound like fun. Suppose you once were Queen Ann or Louis XIV, and could remember it. Some people say they were and do. The authenticity of these memories of past lives is, to say the least, dubious. Most people are suspicious of anyone who remembers a former life. Thinking that you once were Napoleon is not as bad, however, as thinking that you are now Napoleon. In either case, if you persist in bothering people about it, you will likely find that your next migration is to the funny farm.

One view of the transmigration of souls is that when the body dies, the soul moves on to a higher or lower order animal's body depending on how well that soul behaved in its previous body. A soul that made a human body into a glutton might be moved on to be the soul of a pig, whereas the soul of a valorous pig might be moved up to a human. In these merit-system transmigration theories, some god would have to do the judging and implanting. It could not be the Judeo-Christian-Muslim God, because for that God, every soul uniquely inhabits only one human body.

Another view is that it is a free-for-all. In this model, hordes of disembodied souls are said to hover around pregnant women (and other pregnant animals), jockeying for position to possess the newborn living bodies. But how one immaterial soul could push another aside, or get into position, or, for that matter, enter a newborn, is inexplicable. The view that there is a swarming horde of souls fighting to enter the body of every newborn makes no sense because souls are immaterial and unextended. Like the angels on the head of a pin, no one of them can be in a better position than any other to enter a newborn. Furthermore, they have no ability to do anything until they are in a body, so how would they go about making an entry? There is a chicken and egg problem here. These disembodied souls must have the ability to act if they are to enter a body, but they must be in a body to have the ability to act. So the swarming souls theory is impossible. This would seem to support the biblical doctrine that God inserts souls in bodies. They cannot insert themselves.

The more common view is that God implants souls into fetuses. The views of the Catholic Church about when God puts a soul in a human body have varied at different times. Most generally, it is said that God inserts a soul in the embryo when it is "sufficiently developed." This is much too vague, and for a while Catholic doctrine was that boys were given souls twenty days after conception, and girls after forty days. That might suggest that abortion is OK until the souls are implanted. Would it be murder—or even worth notice—if a human embryo without a soul were aborted? Of course even a soulless embryo has the potential to be a full human being. So it makes sense to say that it should be treated with respect.

Recent (1999) Catholic dictionaries say that each soul is created by God at conception. This view is motivated by the abortion controversy. But what about sperm alone and ova alone? Separated sperm and ova would seem far enough down the line that they could be wasted, or, say, used for medical research.

The forty-day criterion came from Aristotle. This was supposed to be the point at which an embryo quickens, that is, when it first moves. Even then Aristotle said only boys became human at forty days. Girls became human only after eighty days. Obviously, Aristotle would think that research on embryos is OK, at least up to forty days from conception.

There is a far-out psychological theory that the soul or self does not appear in a human body until a child recognizes itself. That is, to have a soul, to be yourself, you must be conscious of your self. Some people remember exactly when they realized for the first time that they were separate from other people and things. In psychological literature, Herbert Spiegleberg refers to this as the I-am-me experience. Suddenly you realize that you are you. I never had this experience, or at least I do not remember it. In teaching introduction to philosophy, I sometimes asked the students (who were usually around eighteen years old) if they have had an I-am-me experience. About one out of a dozen do remember their first consciousness of themselves. Children become conscious of themselves as early as age three and as late as age seven. Do these children not have souls until then? If a child does not have a soul until it has that experience, would infanticide be OK up to that point? Is it murder to kill something that does not have a soul? Or that does not know itself? Oysters presumably do not know themselves, and we eat them alive. Lobsters presumably do not have souls, and we boil them alive. A major justification for killing non-human animals for food and other uses is that they do not have souls. Which also means that they have no self-consciousness nor any feelings. So far as I know, among reasons sometimes given for justifying infanticide (terrible deformities, incurable diseases, not enough food to feed more children, too many girls), lack of a soul is not one of them. But not being a Christian or not being a Muslim or being a Jew has more than once been given as a reason for killing someone.

Plato's student Aristotle said that the soul is the form of a living human body. This form is a structural plan of the body that has the power to give a body its size and shape and abilities. Thus one's soul is not a material thing, but is rather both the pattern and the driving force that determines the activities of one's body in rational, human ways. When this force is in action, a self emerges that is conscious of its own personhood. So far so good. But the moment a human body is disorganized by death, the soul that was its driving force disappears and the person with it. There is no immortality of the soul for Aristotle.

In the thirteenth century, Saint Thomas Aquinas followed Aristotle to teach that the soul is the driving force of the body. God unites it with the human body to make a person. But unlike Aristotle, Saint Thomas held the Christian view that the soul survives the death of the body.

Some people think that this notion of the soul as an Aristotelian form has an expression in very contemporary—and non-miraculous—terms. They suggest that the soul is merely a program (plan) for the operation of the human brain and body viewed as a personal computer. When the program is activated in the brain, a self-conscious person emerges.

The soul as a program seems to open up a lot of possibilities. Suppose you could figure out what the program of your soul is and write it up. You could put it on a disk and wait for technology to develop to the stage where we can construct robots, or even manufacture human bodies, that have brains like ours. They would be empty brains. Then the program of your mind (soul) could be downloaded into one of those blank brains, a button punched, and presto! There you would come up conscious on the screen of your new brain and body. But wait. Just your program would not be enough. Then you might appear anew in the world just like a newborn babe. All of your old memories and predilections would have to be recorded too, and downloaded into your new brain. Only when they are activated would you know that you are the same old you.

There are logic-chopping objections to this scheme. Supposing it is successful, the new being would not be the old you, but rather would be an entirely new person that through technological shenanigans merely has the memories of the old you. But this objection is really too refined to worry about. If the downloaded soul thinks like you, remembers what you have done, if it quacks like the duck you were, then it *is* you. Never mind that there might be a gap of several centuries while your program was in storage. You can just chalk that up to a good long night's sleep.

This is, details adjusted, almost identical to the Christian doctrine of the Resurrection. If you are saved, when you die your soul will be put in limbo, then at the end of time your body will be resurrected. Some versions are that it will even be improved. No weaknesses or debilitating diseases will be reconstituted in the cleansed body. You might even be better looking than you were before. Your soul in this reconstituted body would of course remember what happened to you in your earlier life, and you would be you.

Sad to say, the notion that the soul is a program does not work at all. A program is not really an existing thing. It is merely a set of relations or steps expressed in symbols, for example patterns of marks on paper or bits on a disk. A program is just the way the marks or bits are ordered. Thus a program is only a design. In itself it is not even a plan or blueprint, because it must be interpreted by someone who takes it to be a plan or blueprint. A program is something designed to be a guide for various operations in a computer, such as adding, or formatting a paragraph.

Here is the crucial point. A program is just a set of instructions. It is not something that either understands those instructions or that can by itself carry out those instructions. One must have a computer to do this. For those who propose that the mind or soul is a program, the computer they have in mind is the human brain. But not even a computer brain is enough. The critical problem now with the notion that the mind is a program and the brain is a computer is that a programmed computer requires *someone* to program and use it. A computer cannot program itself, nor can a programmed computer operate itself because it is not self-conscious or self-activating. A computer is just a machine that has been designed to accept programs for undertaking certain tasks, such as addition. Someone must insert the program and operate the computer. Even an operating programmed computer is not operating itself. Someone operates it, and that someone is a self-conscious person, not the computer in which the program is being run.

Thus, while the soul might have a pattern that can be duplicated in a program, the pattern or program alone has no power or force and thus cannot activate a computer even if that computer is a human brain. If the brain is a computer, it must be activated by an actor, by someone. The person or self or soul or mind as we conceive it is something that has the power to act. A soul can use a brain and body. It can operate them and act through them. The mere program of a soul cannot.

Of course if scientists in the future can construct living human bodies with empty brains, then presumably they could insert mind programs in them. For Christians, there would be no problem with this because for them God is going to do it during the Resurrection.

An Aristotelian form is defined as just the sort of thing that does have the power to act on matter. Again, the Aristotelian rational soul is very like the Christian soul that Descartes was trying to save—with his dualism of mind and body —for Western philosophy and religion. But such a powerful, independent soul cannot be captured or expressed as merely an un-embodied abstract pattern or plan or program. The essence of such a soul is its power to think and act.

The immortal soul we yearn for is a self-acting something. It is a something so powerful and real that it can exist through all eternity. It is an immaterial substance that persists and survives the crash of that personal computer to which your mother gave birth. Nothing like it is known to modern science.

But the brain does seem to be programmed. It can do many things that our selves have not programmed into it. For example, I have learned how to read and write, abilities I was not born with. You could say that my teachers took me through some routines that resulted in my brain being programmed so I can read and write. But language scientists today believe that humans are born with capacities to learn these things. I could not be programmed to read and write unless my brain were set up to run such programs.

I can do many things that I was never taught. For example, I can run and jump and throw rocks. Using the metaphor of the computer, scientists sometimes say that human brains and bodies were programmed in the process of evolution through interaction with the natural environment. On this materialist view, there is no independent soul or self that operates the body machine. The body and its mind-brain is self-operating (as the computers we construct are not). What does the body do? It reacts to the environment to survive. When it dies, it's dead. That's all. So even if a soul were a program in the brain, it would disintegrate when the body does.

Another view held by many in both the East and the West is that there is a world soul, or even that the entire universe is a thinking, personal being. You and I—our souls—are little pips in the plasma of this eternal world soul. The nineteenth-century philosopher Hegel had the notion that this world soul was just coming to consciousness. Self-consciousness was appearing in little globs here and there in superior intellects such as his own, mostly in the Germany of his time. Our job is to help the world soul come to consciousness.

Hegel's fragmented world spirit fighting to unite and come to consciousness is something like the will-to-be that Schopenhauer said all things have, except that for Hegel, coming to consciousness is a process of unification, whereas for Schopenhauer, the will-to-be is permanently fragmented into untold numbers of mostly unconscious, uncooperating, antagonistic spiritual powers and forces. They are out to eliminate one another. Kill the competition! But Schopenhauer does not explain how these powers operate living bodies.

As for the theory that there is a world soul, the problem is that on this view, our individual personal selves are merely parts or aspects of the as yet partial self-consciousness of the world soul. Once the world soul becomes fully conscious, the differences between deluded selves such as yours and mine will disappear. All of us individual souls yearning for eternal life will find it when the world soul balloons out into total consciousness. But this eternal life will be won at the price of the loss of our own souls and individual selves through merging into the one world soul. Once again, this is not what we had in mind.

In the Buddhist version of this universal soul, there is no ultimate self-consciousness at all. There is just an infinite ocean of consciousless Nirvana. Our self-consciousness is a delusion, so we should meditate to get rid of it. Our personal selves with all our concerns, trials, and tribulations should be shunned and scorned. We must learn to think of nothing to become nothing. Our greatest pleasures even more than our greatest pains are the greatest hindrances to our attainment of sublime eternity. Only when we escape consciousness of our personal selves through deprivation and meditation can we merge with the infinite. Once again, however, this eternity is not at all what we had in mind. To disappear like a raindrop in the ocean is not the ordinary person's idea of a Heavenly good time.

Most people, including philosophers and scientists, do not want to disappear at death. We want to find out what happens next. We want to continue the story. We have a lot of unfinished things to do and that we want to know. Because we think that our souls are our selves, we would like our souls to survive our deaths. But if our soul-minds are our brains, we're out of here. Soon.

Here is our litany. It is like prayer. If we repeat it often enough, we might even begin to believe that our wants could come true.

O Big Bang! (Or, if you wish: Oh God!)
May we retain our memories and our power to feel and think
and do forever.
May we remember our past lives.
May we meet with the souls of our loved ones who are
deceased.
And may we have the power to do what we want to
do with whomever and wherever we want to do it.
In a word, when we are dead, may we be just as we are now,
except without a body.

But there is a major flaw in this. Lack of a body gives rise to an incredibly difficult, apparently insoluble problem. After death, a soul has no body. It has no sense organs, so how can it have sensory experiences? It has no brain, so how can it think? The brain is where memories are stored, so how can a disembodied soul remember anything? It cannot remember even who it is, or, perhaps, one should say, it cannot remember even who it was. Nor can it imagine anything because imagination too depends on the brain. Moreover, because this poor soul has no body, it cannot act on other bodies. It cannot speak to others, or gesture to them, or touch them. It cannot send e-mail. Nobody living has ever heard from anyone who is dead. Sure, there are all sorts of stories about people getting messages from their deceased loved ones. None of them has ever been authenticated. One problem is that when a dead soul in a dream does tell where the lost diamond ring is, when added in with the number of dreams that make no sense, this success is often statistically less than would be expected from a random search. How about consulting a Ouija board? Look, there is no way an immaterial spirit could push that little three-legged platform around.

Even if a disembodied soul could know itself, how could it know any other soul? How could one soul contact another soul? You and I contact one another by talking or writing. But a soul without a body cannot talk or write.

In life, virtually all our concerns are based in our bodies. As

Descartes was not the first to point out, what we most need and desire in life is good bodily health. This precedes contentment of mind. We need food, clothing, shelter, and security—for our bodies. We work to satisfy our desires, almost all of which are based in our bodies.

There is, for example, sexual pleasure, which Sigmund Freud said was the basis of our dreams of paradise. The desire, no, the demand for satisfaction of our sexual desires, is as intense as any feeling or drive or passion we have. It is driven by our hormones, and diminishes greatly when their production is reduced.

Here is the question: What would bodily health and satisfaction amount to after death? Alas, the Muslim Heaven full of concubines (a notion obviously thought up by a man) would be totally without interest to a disembodied soul. Only the body has hormones. But the Muslim Heaven shows that we want to have a sensory life after death. This is impossible without sense organs. No wonder the resurrection of the body has been a part of religions from the ancient Egyptians to present-day Christians. As remarked above, Heaven would not be much fun, nor would Hell fires torment, unless we had bodies. How can you feel anything if you cannot touch, or be touched by, it?

We have before us, then, not merely a question of what one could or would do without a body. There is also the question of what a soul would *want* to do if it had no body. Without any bodily desires or sensory feelings, a lot is ruled out. One answer is that our souls, purified by their separation from the body, would spend eternity contemplating and worshiping God. Why else would God save our souls? So instead of praying for a resurrected body, why not get prepared to leave the one you have? Obviously, the body's desires are the greatest hindrance to beatitude.

There is a strong element of asceticism in almost all religions including Christianity. The ascetic way to salvation is to scorn and scourge one's body, deprive it of all satisfaction of its desires, chastise it, and eventually overcome and transcend it to worship and effect union with God.

This ascetic view of the body is a major foundation of the establishment of celibate priests and nuns in the Catholic Church.

As to what a disembodied soul that reaches the ultimate stage is or does or thinks, no one can say because it is beyond sensory experience. So asceticism merges with mysticism. The ascetic reaches a mystical realm in which one loses one's self. Mystics strive to reach this stage while still alive. A problem here is that if a mystic does reach the stage of transcendence of self in this life, he or she (or it?) will not know it because the previous self is transcended in the experience. Of course if transcendence of self happens after one dies, one will not know it then either.

Descartes was fully aware of these problems. Like Plato, he thought disembodied souls could certainly think, but not about particular things. The dead can think only about general ideas. Again, consider the experiences we have when our bodies interact with the world about us. All our sensory experiences are about particular things because they come to us only through the actions of particular bodies on our sense organs. We see only when light waves hit our eyes, hear only when sound waves reach our ears. We experience tastes and smells only when something touches our tongues and when volatile atoms stimulate the membranes in our noses. Touch is not possible without a body to be touched.

Moreover, a disembodied soul or mind can neither remember nor imagine sensory experiences. Both memory and imagination require the mind to instigate activity in the brain like that ordinarily caused by the nerve actions that follow impacts on our sense organs. When you remember or imagine your mother's face, for example, you cause brain activity similar to that which occurs when your mother is actually standing in front of you and light rays are reflected from her face onto your retina. This causes nerve activity that stimulates the brain and then you are aware of an image of her face. Your memory can revive or reconstruct this image in your imagination. You can use your imagination to bring up images in almost any order you wish.

But a disembodied soul has no access to a brain, so it can neither remember its former experiences nor imagine anything at all. So how would you know who you are after you have left your body? You—your mind or soul—would be the same one it always was, but without memories, you would have no continuity with the past, like someone with total amnesia. So would that really be you?

Descartes was one of the first to describe correctly how we

perceive the world of material things. They act on our sense organs that send messages through the nerves to cause brain activity that results in our having sensations and ideas of those material things. Our particular experiences make unique impressions on our brains (program them, if you will) so each of us can retrieve or reconstruct images and ideas as memories and also manipulate them in imagination. The point is that the particular person and personality that you are is generated by your bodily experience. Each person's body and experience are unique. Descartes realized that when the soul is separated from its body and brain at death and in effect becomes a disembodied mind, all that uniqueness is lost. The *particular* experiences one has had and stored as memories in one's brain are gone.

So a disembodied soul thinks of God? The Judeo-Christian-Muslim God is omnipotent, omniscient, omnipresent, perfect, and good. But no one has ever claimed that the human mind can actually understand the nature of these attributes. When one says God is good, one does not and cannot mean the same thing as when one says that a human being is good. This has led to the view that one can think of God only in terms of negative attributes, e.g., God is not evil, God is not a deceiver, God is not weak, and so on. But this way of thinking of God obviously does not lead to any positive knowledge about God. It leads only to knowledge of what God is not.

It is not surprising, then, that mystics who think they have made contact with God or merged with God have difficulty in describing the experience. Often they say that there was a feeling of oneness with the universe, or that they saw a bright light, or that they had an experience of a vast vacancy or of emptiness or of nothing. The boundaries between their selves and the universe dissolve. In Chapter One above, I quote a description of such an experience had by Ursula Goodenough. Those who have it lose themselves in this experience. If our personal selves are tied to our bodies, maybe we do meld into the infinite whole when we separate from our bodies as mystics claim to do. But once again, this is not what most of us have in mind when we yearn for the afterlife. Contemplating an infinite that is vacuous and unintelligible is not most people's idea of Heaven.

Nevertheless, some of the brightest people who have ever thought about the problem have concluded that the fate of disembodied souls is eternal contemplation of the unknown and unknowable God. If that is unsatisfactory to ordinary people—and it is—theologians dumb down the message. God's ways are beyond us. We are not to worry. We may not understand these matters, but everything will come out all right. This is what Descartes told Princess Elisabeth. She was not consoled.

The evangelical Christian way of handling the problem is to say that at the end of time, God will resurrect every born again soul's body. That solves the problem of your being yourself and remembering who you were when you were alive. Your resurrected body would also give you many particular things to think about, that is, everything that happened to you when you were alive. In Heaven, you could meet and interact with all your deceased loved ones, just as you used to do on earth.

This seems to be what most people want. The problem with it is that it is not a solution to the problem of what a *disembodied* soul does in the afterlife. Resurrection is just a return to one's body. One is resurrected to life as we know it now except that everything is nicer in Heaven. Resurrectionists just want to return to life as we know it, only better. This doctrine is understandably very popular, but is it anything more than wishful thinking?

Even if the problems of inserting a soul in a body at birth, and of resurrecting a body after death, were solved, the problem of how mind and body interact remains. If the mind or soul is never manifested except in union with a body and a brain, perhaps the soul is nothing but the brain.

These are difficult matters that most people do not want to worry about. So they put their faith in the supernatural powers of God.

To get a notion of what this faith truly amounts to, consider the explanation offered by Tertullian in the third century A.D. He said that one should believe in Christianity because it is absurd. I do not pretend to understand what this means. Saint Ignatius Loyola, who founded the Jesuits in the sixteenth century, said that when you can actually believe that snow is black, then you can be a true Christian. The nineteenth-century philosopher Søren Kierkegaard said that the craziest thing he could think of is that Jesus died for his (Kierkegaard's) sins. So he believed in Christianity.

Blaise Pascal, Descartes's younger contemporary and, like Descartes, a genius mathematician, was terrified at the prospects of Hell. Nevertheless, he had difficulty accepting the absurdity of Christianity. So for himself and for others who have trouble believing, he proposed what has become known as Pascal's Wager. If, he said, God exists and you do not believe, you go to Hell, and that is losing a lot. But if you believe, and it turns out that God does not exist, you have lost nothing. So the smart gambler—Pascal, like Descartes, had figured out the odds and won a lot of money playing cards believes in God.

Of course one cannot believe something merely by deciding to believe it, as Humpty Dumpty claimed he could do. For people who want to believe in Christianity but find it difficult to do so, Pascal proposed the following routine. Go to mass every day and go through all the ceremonies. Do this for, say, eighteen years. One day, lo and behold, you will wake up a believer.

The serious flaw in these proposals is that the options are not simply either believing or not believing in Christianity. That is to assume that Christianity is the true religion. But what about all the other gods and religions? One must begin with the belief that Christianity is the only possibly true religion. It does, however, promise what many people want—resurrection of the body and eternal life.

Chapter 4.

Angels and Ghosts

The origin of the word "angel" is the Greek word for "messenger." Virtually all religions have angels (messengers from the gods) and ghosts or spirits of the dead. Angels come first. In biblical tradition, there are nine kinds of angels in three choirs:

Seraphim
Cherubim
Virtues

Powers
Principalities
Dominions

Thrones
Archangels
Angels

An issue that Saint Thomas Aquinas discussed in the thirteenth century is whether or not for each kind of angel, there are numerous individuals of that kind, or only one individual for each kind. The question arises as follows.

Consider beagle hounds as a kind of dog. There are many individual dogs of that type. My father raised beagles (my brother Jim had one named Hector), and I can assure you that while all beagle hounds have certain characteristics in common, such as a passion for chasing rabbits, each is different in its own way—just like you and me. Is it the same for angels of the same type?

Given that angels have no bodies, angels cannot differ as you and I do by having different bodily constitutions. These bodily differences provide us with different experiences of the world. Our bodily constitutions also determine differences in our personalities. Angels differ in type, that is, according to which of the nine kinds a given angel exemplifies. But angels of a given type do not have bodies to individuate them. Nor do angels of a given type differ according to personality. Angels of a given type are differentiated by each one having different, unique, particular experiences that differ from the experiences of all the other angels of that type.

Angels differ in kind, and angels of a given kind differ on the basis of their different experiences.

But there is another view, that there is only one individual of each type of angel. The argument for this is that if there were two angels of the same type, they would be exactly alike and so could not differ in any way. Leibniz presented this metaphysical view in his principle of the identity of indiscernibles. Two things that are exactly alike in all ways are really only one thing. So this view is that if you know one angel of a given type, you know them all (of that type).

This result leads to the heresy of angelism, which was pointed out by Saint Gregory of Nyssa in the fourth century. Saint Gregory reasoned that human beings are individuated from one another only by their different bodies and worldly experiences. Thus when a human soul is disengaged from its body at death, there is nothing to individuate it from any other disembodied human soul. Every disembodied human soul is exactly like every other disembodied human soul—just as each angel of a given type is exactly like all other angels of that type (if there should be more than one angel of each type). And so, some argued that given that disembodied human souls cannot be distinguished from one another, there is really only one human soul, and this soul is an angel. This is viewed by the Church as the heresy of angelism.

Let's check the crucial logical point here. If you were told about two different things that were exactly like one another in all respects, wouldn't you begin to suspect that there is only one thing under discussion? Here is a standard philosopher's example. Consider the book you are now holding. If there were seventeen individual books exactly like this one, all in exactly the same place at the same time, how would you be able to tell that there were seventeen rather than only one? Or seventeen million? The only way of distinguishing, say, identical twins, is by observing them side-by-side. But the supposed seventeen books—all entirely alike in all ways—cannot be separated side-by-side (because one of the ways they are exactly like one another is by all being in the same place). So the most reasonable thing to conclude is that there are not seventeen books in your hand, but only one.

But wait. If each book weighed one pound, then seventeen books would weigh seventeen pounds, and if all of them were in your hand at once, you would certainly know it. OK. But since angels weigh nothing, you couldn't tell the difference between one and seventeen of them by weight. As far as that goes, angels have no extension, so not even one of them could be in a place, let alone many of them in the same place (as I have already discussed concerning angels on the head of a pin). Which all goes to show again that immaterial angels of the same type cannot be distinguished from one another the way material bodies are. Neither can disembodied human souls be so distinguished according to Gregory of Nyssa.

The kinds of angels differ in their knowledge and powers. Two or more angels that have the same knowledge and powers cannot be distinguished from one another, because they have no other characteristics except their knowledge and powers. But couldn't two angels of the same type differ in their experiences? Again no, because angels do not and cannot have experiences. Experiences are particular and they result from bodily interactions. Angels don't have bodies and they don't have bodily interactions. So not only do angels not differ according to their experiences, they can't even have experiences. The conclusion again is that there is only one angel of each kind.

To differ, two angels of the same kind would—like human souls—have to be united with bodies that differ from one another in constitution, in their place and motion, and in their interactions with other bodies. Only then could you say there were two angels of the same kind. Of course there are some people who say that this happens.

But suppose angelism is after all true of the human soul, that there is only one human soul. This soul is fractionated somehow so that each fraction has all the powers and attributes of the whole soul. God associates each fraction with a different human body. But when a human body dies, there is no individual soul to be released. Instead, the soul-fraction that was united to that body merely rejoins the one (and only) human soul.

Probably one should say that the soul-fraction simply remains the one human soul. But how can a part be equal to the whole? It cannot. The notion of fractionating, then, is only a metaphor. There is no explanation for how one soul could spread itself through many human bodies in such a way that each of us thinks he or she has a unique and independent soul. Anyway, fractionation requires division. But only extended bodies can be divided into parts. The one angelic human soul would be unextended. So it makes no sense to talk of fractionating the soul. Thus angelism makes no sense. The conclusion from this is that there is a different human soul for each body.

But maybe not. Suppose again that angelism were true. If there were only one human soul, then when a human being dies, the fraction that was its soul would rejoin the one soul. This would be a result like that popularly ascribed to Eastern religions in which one's soul at death is said to unite with a world soul and thus lose all the individuality and identity it had when it was joined in life to a human body. According to the doctrines both of angelism and generally speaking of Buddhism and Hinduism, the personality of which each of us is now conscious is an illusion brought on by the soul's association with a body. So you and I, as self-conscious minds or souls, are illusions. We disappear when our bodies die. We have reached another dead end.

The Fathers of the Catholic Church rejected angelism. After the Resurrection when one's soul is reunited with one's body, one becomes conscious of oneself. Only then can one enjoy the pleasures of Heaven or suffer the pains of Hell. Souls combined with bodies feel things. Disembodied souls do not.

The question now is: Can disembodied souls move about in the world? Can they be perfect tourists who go in an instant wherever they want, to enjoy the sights without the agony of travel? Alas, no. The dwelling place of disembodied souls is bleak. It really is not a place at all. Dead souls can't walk and they can't talk. Perhaps this is why it has never been demonstrated that any dead soul has made contact with a living person. The reason is that there is no possible way that a disembodied soul could make contact with a living person.

But the Bible tells us that angels move about and see what is going on in the world and the Archangel Gabriel is said to have talked with David, Jesus, and Mohammed. The bad angel Satan tempted Christ, tormented Job, and creates havoc regularly on earth. The good angel Michael battles Satan to protect us.

There are many stories about angels appearing to people. Angels—and even God, Jesus, and the Virgin Mary—have appeared to some people (so these people say) to tell them things or to give them support just as they were about to fall off a cliff. These spirits or apparitions are supposed to have the ability not only to move about in the world, but also to see (and be seen) and to talk, and help or harm people. Only if they help are they called angels. If they harm, they are called demons.

Can angels (and demons) actually assume bodily form? They would have to if they talk, or give people a helping hand, or stick pins in them, or have sexual relations with them as incubi and succubae are said to do. Only beings with material bodies can do these things.

The standard way an immaterial being such as an angel or a demon is said to control bodies is not by pushing them around directly, but by acting directly on a human mind to cause that mind to move its body the way the angel or demon desires. If a demon wants a rock thrown at someone, the demon cannot do this directly. What it must do is coerce a mind to have the body to which it is united throw the rock. Can a demon actually do this?

There is a huge literature about demons taking over human bodies. Demons possess people by entering their bodies and controlling their minds. They speak inside people's minds to tell them to do things. Sometimes they pretend they are angels or Jesus or God. Demons also are said to control human bodies by shoving aside human souls and taking over. In Descartes's day, there was a famous case at Loudun in France where demons were thought to have taken over the bodies of some girls in a convent school. The demons made these girls say blasphemous things and contort their bodies lewdly. Belief in demonic possession is strong today as shown by how many people take novels and movies such as *The Exorcist* seriously.

The way an immaterial being such as an angel or a demon controls bodies, then, is not by pushing them around, but by acting directly on a human mind to cause that mind to move its body the way the angel or demon desires.

People possessed by demons do all sorts of things they would not otherwise do. They blaspheme, engage in lewd and lascivious behavior, pinch people, and in general make an awful nuisance of themselves. But of course, you are not yourself if you are possessed by a demon. To regain control of yourself and your body, the demon must be expelled or exorcised. In the Bible, Jesus cast out a batch of demons that had possessed two men by driving the demons into a herd of swine. These pigs then rushed into the sea where they were drowned, and the demons flew off in a rage. A dead body is of no use to a demon.

Drowning the possessed, of course, is not the preferred way to exorcise a demon. On the other hand, pigs don't have Christian souls. Drowning actually was, for many centuries, a popular way of determining whether or not someone was a witch. The theory is simple. If the woman is possessed by a demon, then the demon will protect her from drowning. A lot of old women were absolved of being witches by being held under water for ten minutes or so.

Can angels or demons really take over a human mind? How would they go about doing it? People who are possessed say that they hear voices in their heads. If they think the voices come from God or Jesus, they often obey the voices. But if they think the voices come from demons or Satan, they try to resist the suggestions. Nevertheless, the demons sometimes deceive or overpower them, causing them to do bad things. The fact is, people who hear voices they believe are from God, Jesus, or angels also do bad things. In 1978, the Reverend Jones of the Jonesville cult believed that God wanted him and his disciples to commit suicide. So Jones laced Kool-Aid with cyanide, and 912 people including 276 children either committed suicide or were murdered.

Nobody denies that some people hear voices. Suppose such a person does what the voices say—whether or not he thinks the voices are from good or bad angels—and does something terrible. If that person is brought to trial, what do we do? Often we decide that the perpetrator is insane. Medical treatment, not exorcism, is prescribed.

What if the perpetrator does not remember doing the awful thing? What if a bad (or good) angel pushes a person's self or soul aside and takes over that person's body entirely? Then the demon, say, has full control of the body. Something like this happens in Robert Louis Stevenson's story of the good Dr. Jekyll and the evil Mr. Hyde. Mr. Hyde takes over Dr. Jekyll's body, and Dr. Jekyll cannot remember a thing Mr. Hyde does during that time. Belief in demonic possession is very common. But how can a living body be subject to takeover by an angel or a demon? And if there were a takeover, what happens to the body's legitimate soul? Where does it go?

How would a takeover be possible? Remember the argument that it would do no good for disembodied souls to try to enter a newborn baby, because disembodied souls have no power to enter a body. Only God can insert a soul in a body. Thus the notion that good or bad angels could take over a living human body makes no sense. As disembodied beings, angels and demons have no power to act on or enter a body. To act on a body, a soul must already be in a body. But despite its seeming impossibility, people often believe that a disembodied soul can push an occupying soul out of a body and take it over. This notion of souls of dead people taking over the bodies of living people leads us to ghosts and demons.

Ghosts are supposed to be the disembodied souls of dead people. Generally the reason they are ghosts is that they have not managed to enter the other world, that is, they have not gotten to Heaven or Hell or paradise or wherever. They are suspended in a limbo between this world and the next. Thus they are said to retain some ties to this world, which is why we can encounter them as ghosts.

Reasons why dead souls become ghosts vary. One is that they have not earned the right to move on, so they have to complete something left undone in their life here. They might, for example, have murdered someone, so have to hang around to try to find someone to forgive them. Or perhaps they themselves have been murdered and the murderer has not yet been caught and punished. Whatever the cause of their between-worlds status, ghosts are usually unhappy. Some of them merely waft about wailing and lamenting. Haunted houses are famous for noisy ghosts. This can be very disconcerting even if these sad ghosts never actually harm anyone. But ghosts often are said to hurt people. In many cultures, if you annoy a ghost, it can do you a lot of harm. Some mean ghosts are said to kill people, or to drive them mad, or even to eat them. Incubi and succubae, who have sexual relations with people while they sleep, are sometimes thought of as ghosts. Often they carry out these acts in most unpleasant ways.

The ancient Egyptians had very elaborate notions concerning ghosts. They believed that for the soul to survive death, the body had to be preserved as perfectly as possible. They did this by mummifying bodies, as every child knows. The reason for mummification is that they believed that the soul had to have access to its former body so that it would remember who it was. Moreover, the ghost had to be fed and provided with water to drink. Other objects of use, such as combs, footstools, and even pets (which were killed and also embalmed) had to be provided. If the deceased was an important man, his favorite bull and his servants were killed and mummified to be on hand to please and serve him.

The ancient Egyptians thought that if they did not do these things, the ghost or spirit of the dead man would forget who he was and go howling through an empty cosmos. The Mummy's Curse—a threat that the ghost of the mummy will kill whoever disturbs the mummy— sounds great, but in fact it was made up by journalists when Howard Carter was excavating King Tut's tomb in 1922. Since then, The Mummy's Curse has appeared in thousands of stories, novels, comic books, movies, and television shows, and surely will never die. But there is no evidence that the ancient Egyptians thought that a lost ghost would or could harm anyone. They paid attention to the dead out of compassion. Only if the spirit was kept aware of who it was, and only if it was carefully attended to would it survive as a personality. What a lost spirit amounted to for the ancient Egyptians was either virtually nothing, or perhaps a well of fear and horror and sadness.

The first Europeans to enter the southeastern part of North America did find that when an important man died among the Natchez Indians, they killed young women to go along to serve the spirit of the dead man. A thousand years ago in what is now Illinois at the confluence of the Missouri and Mississippi Rivers at Cahokia,

102

the largest prehistoric site north of Mexico, when one great man died, twenty young women and a dozen other people were killed to serve him after death.

In the Hindu religion, when a man dies, his wife is supposed to perform Suttee, which is the act of committing suicide by leaping into the flames of his funeral pyre to be burned up with him. Souls after death for Hindus ordinarily transmigrate to other living bodies. But the good woman who commits Suttee (Suttee means good woman) may have gained enough virtuous points in the form of karma so that her soul merges with the infinite, which is the ultimate goal in Hinduism.

A ghost, then, is not always thought of as something harmful that is to be feared. Some of them call for compassion. Others—American Indian religions are famous for these—can be called on as guardian spirits. At this point, the Fairy Godmother stage, ghosts and angels merge into Disneyland fantasies.

Where do people get the idea that there are ghosts and demons, anyway? Most likely from dreams. In dreams we see images of dead people, we interact with them, and they seem to be very much present and alive. We may even realize in the dreams that they are dead, and think they are communicating with us from the great beyond. It is a small step from dream images to ghosts. They are equally insubstantial.

Where people fear ghosts and demons, the banishment of ghosts and the exorcism of demons are big business. Witch doctors and priests are required to ward off their evil effects.

The worst thing ghosts can do is occupy living human bodies. They do this in an attempt to live again. I have already examined this possibility in the discussion of angels and demons. It does not seem possible that these immaterial beings could have the power to take over a body. But supposedly if you are very tired or incautious, a ghost might just push you out and occupy your body. Or a demon sneak in. Again, we know of no comprehensible way that this could take place. The reputation ghosts have for being filmy and insubstantial—you can put your hand right through them—has good grounds in the general notion of disembodied souls as not having any physical or material substantiality at all. But this also rules out comic-book ghosts as sheets with holes for eyes, because immaterial ghosts cannot have a location and cannot be seen. If tellers of tales were restricted to this strict notion of ghosts, a lot of ghost stories would be ruined.

These great cosmic stories—of angels watching over us and demons possessing us, of ghosts, of one world spirit coming to consciousness, of untold billions of bodiless spirits attempting to enter the bodies of newborn babies—are marvelously entertaining. They have also been enormously influential in Judaism, Christianity, and Islam. In these religions, you pray to God to help you. Or, if you are a cynic, you worship the devil, as do the Yezidi in Iraq. Their view is: Why worry about God? God is good and no threat (although one wonders how well they have read the Bible or the Koran if they believe this). In any case, the Yezidi and other self-styled devil worshippers say it is only reasonable to propitiate Satan. In all these religions, spiritual entities such as angels, ghosts, and demons are out there to help or harm you. They represent or depend upon good and evil forces in the universe.

In Eastern religions, there is also a notion of a neutral spiritual force in the universe that can be tapped. Sometimes this is called karma. But to consider it in all its contemporary, secular, technological glory, just think of the immense popularity of the Star Wars movies in which the powers of light are pitched against the powers of darkness. The force is there, it may be with you, if you concentrate in the right way, or, as my father used to say, if you hold your mouth right. Again, the force is neutral. Both good and evil beings can gain access to it.

To begin considering that force, suppose, as Schopenhauer did, that the activating force in nature is will power. Each of us has such a power. This will power allows us to transform or redirect energy. For example, my left arm is stretched out on my writing table as determined by the general laws of nature. If I want to raise it, my soul or mind has the ability (I've just done it) to engage and redirect the energy in the physical situation of my arm on the table so that my arm rises up in the air. That's what it feels like to raise one's arm, that is, you just decide to do it and it is done. Deciding is actually not enough. You direct your arm to rise.

Leibniz claimed that Descartes had a similar theory. Descartes, Leibniz said, did not think the soul could generate force, but rather that the soul could redirect force. You cannot change the quantity of force, but you can decide its direction of thrust. This supposedly would not interfere with the deterministic interaction of bodies. But that is wrong, as Leibniz and Newton pointed out. Not only the force but also the direction of movement is fully determined by past movements or causes. What is required is a power to reach into the determined situation and rearrange its determination. You must have the ability to alter the determined course of events. I have no idea how such a force would work, but as Descartes pointed out to Princess Elisabeth, we all experience our ability to do it.

That we do not know how a force works is fatal neither to its proposal nor to its action. The fact is that we do not know how the force of gravity works either, but we see that it does work. There are proposals about how the force of electromagnetism works, and the weak and strong nuclear forces. But what powers these forces, what generates them, what fuels them, what causes them, nobody knows. Of course the Big Bang released a lot of energy. But why did the Big Bang release energy in the form of those forces? Or how? And why do they work the way they do? And so on. No one knows. We know what happens, but not why. So the question is: Scientists can handle "what?" questions, that is, questions of what happens. But will we ever know the answer to "why?" questions?

The eighteenth-century philosopher David Hume said no, we will never know the answers to "why?" questions because they are silly questions in the precise sense that they are meaningless. He proposed a theory of force and causation that is widely accepted by philosophers and scientists today. Hume asks you to observe a white billiard ball hitting a red billiard ball on a table. You observe that the white one stops and the red one moves on. But did you observe any force? Any causation? No, all you saw was a white ball rolling up to touch the red ball at which point the white ball stops and the red ball starts rolling. Force and causation, if they exist at all, are unobservable. All you can observe is a sequence of events. What you see is what follows what. The same is true for any sequence of events, even an explosion. You don't see the power or force of dynamite, you just see, for example, a wall of rock that suddenly collapses into a pile of stones. The most we observe in nature, then, is what follows what.

Hume said that what we call natural laws are simply generalizations from our experience of what commonly follows what. We describe what happens and talk of forces that cause these things to happen. But, for example, the law of falling bodies is just a way of describing in mathematical terms what happens when a material body is unsupported. We say it is in the grip of the force of gravity. But in fact, although we see and feel things falling, these experiences do not show us any forces or causes. The point is just that what happens, happens. Period. That's all she (Mother Nature) wrote. That's all there is. We know how, but not why. We see events, but not causes. So causal forces are nothing but our words for the regular way material bodies interact. Hume's final word is that it makes no sense to ask why something happens. There is no why. There is only what happens—what follows what.

When we propose a force or power of will to explain how we move our bodies about, that would be no different from proposing a force of gravity to explain why bodies fall. Or from proposing electromagnetic forces and weak and strong nuclear forces to explain other consistent physical relations among things in the material world. In each of these cases, what we do is give general descriptions of what regularly happens in the world, and postulate forces that cause these happenings. This is all we can do.

The same goes for proposing a force of will to explain why my arm regularly rises when I direct it to do so. The fact that my arm rises whenever I direct it to do so is plain enough. It happens often. But there is no evidence for postulating a power of free will to explain this, nor, as Hume points out, is there any need to do so. We can still use descriptions of regularities—call them laws of nature—to get about in the world as is our habit, but we should not take them to refer to real causes and forces, for there are none.

Hume's argument is very persuasive. We do not perceive forces, we just infer them from what we observe. Most physicists, however, find that the experimental evidence for the force of gravity, electromagnetic forces, and weak and strong nuclear forces is overwhelming. Most people think that the evidence for a force of free will to move our bodies is overwhelming too. However, the evidence for a spiritual force pervading the universe, let alone one we can tap into, is exceedingly sparse. So much for Star Wars. But surely there is something to mind power. Let's look more closely at minds.

Chapter 5.

The Powers of the Mind

The evidence that there are souls or minds is that each of us is certain of the existence of his or her own self-person-mind-soul because he or she is conscious of it. The problem with this evidence is that it is pathetically, even frighteningly, limited. There are long periods of time during which one is not aware of oneself, for example, often when one is asleep. Even when one is awake, one has many periods vacant of self-awareness. For Descartes, the very being of the soul or mind is constituted by its activity of thinking. For him, that one is always thinking means that one is always self-conscious because if one is not self-consciously thinking, then one does not exist. To bridge those vacant periods everyone has both when awake as well as when sleeping, Descartes said one really is self-consciously thinking then, it is just that one's thoughts are so fleeting that one forgets them instantly.

That problem solved, the evidence that there are souls or minds is also limited numerically. This is the frightening part. As a thinking being, you can be certain about the existence of only one thinking being, yourself. Each of us can be quite certain that he or she has a mind or soul, but that's it. You cannot be conscious of other people's selves or thoughts. You can say confidently, "I think, therefore I am" or "I exist," but you can only assume or infer that other people think, so they exist.

Only through reasoning by analogy to your own experience can you support your conviction that living human bodies other than your own are united with thinking minds and thus that each is occupied by a soul or self. These other bodies behave the way you do. They make noises (talk) the way you would if you were them. You ask a friend, "Are you conscious?" and your friend answers, "Of course I am." But computers can be programmed to carry on conversations. So how do you tell the difference?

Descartes proposed a test. He said that the way to tell if something is thinking and thus has a soul is to talk to it long enough to assure yourself that no machine could be engineered to reply as responsively as it does. Descartes believed that only self-conscious thinkers can respond appropriately to whatever might be said to them. In the twentieth century, this became known as the Turing test after the British philosopher and mathematician Alan Turing, who was one of the seminal thinkers in the development of computers. Hide the machine behind a screen, then test to see if people it talks to can figure out that it is a machine. In the seventeenth century, and even in the mid-twentieth century, it seemed reasonable to think that one could tell whether or not one was talking to a machine. Now in the twenty-first century, the technology of computers and the sophistication of programming continue to advance so rapidly that it is no longer fantastic to think that someday a computer will be programmed to talk responsively on all subjects so extensively and apparently spontaneously that no one can tell—just from conversing with it—that it is not a self-conscious living human being.

Even if we could tell, a serious question would remain about whether or not such a machine is not in fact self-conscious. If it were self-conscious, then wouldn't it have a soul? Or would this show that human minds and thus human souls are material just like the mind/soul of a talking computer?

You might remark that some computers can already deceive human beings. If Kasparov, for example, had not been told that Deep Blue was a computer, and they had played their famous chess game by e-mail, he would have thought he had been beaten by a person, not by a computer. In fact, of course, he was not beaten by a computer. He was beaten by the team of human beings who programmed and operated Deep Blue.

For all kinds of mathematical tasks, computers are faster and more reliable than human beings. But computers are not (yet) thinking machines. The thinking is done by the human beings who program the computers to undertake mechanical tasks of computation. Only human beings can interpret the symbols fed into the computers and the symbols the computers spew out. The designs that appear on the computer screen, or the noises the computer makes, are not even words unless designated as such by programmers. They mean something and can be understood by us only because we assign meanings to them. Computers don't know anything. They really are just dumb machines. They don't speak. We speak through them.

This linkage of talking with having a mind or soul that is self-conscious causes serious theological problems, at least in the Judeo-Christian-Muslim tradition. Most of us infer that not just other humans, but also many other animals have minds as we know we do. (Most people are squeamish about saying that nonhuman animals have souls, although saying that they have minds amounts to the same thing.) Chimpanzees and other great apes, dolphins and whales, elephants, and even gray parrots, can understand many things we say to them, and can respond appropriately with sign language, by typing on a computer, by pointing to symbols, or, in the case of parrots, by articulating spoken words. Their subjects are limited and elementary, and much of their conversation concerns food and eating (and in the case of chimpanzees, tickling). But they can add and subtract, identify colors, and work out simple problems in reasoning. A parrot whose name is Alex (who, alas, died young—did he have a soul?) and was studied and taught by Irene Pepperberg, sometimes checked out whether new human acquaintances knew their numbers and colors. Certainly chimpanzees have no hesitation in asking anyone they meet for something to eat.

My friend the poet Donald Finkel and I once visited the primatologist Roger Fouts to meet Washoe, the first chimpanzee to be taught American Sign Language. Donald and I spent a day, each of us in charge of an adolescent chimpanzee with whom we communicated by sign language. They are smart and they know what they want. Mine even tricked me into letting him get away from me. He ran to the moat, jumped into a rowboat, and started rowing across. One of the graduate students plunged in after him and brought him back. He didn't know how to swim and was in danger of drowning if he fell out. (Alas, Donald Finkel died of severe Alzheimer's and did not know at the end even who he was. I looked into his blank face and wondered, is he in there someplace?)

Are chimpanzees self-conscious? What a silly question. My cat Cougar is self-conscious, at least some of the time, and he doesn't begin to be as smart or articulate as a chimpanzee. Furthermore, there are extensive experiments to show that apes and dolphins recognize themselves in mirrors. If a white dot of paint is put on a chimpanzee's forehead while he is sleeping, when he wakes up and looks in a mirror, he instantly reaches up and touches the white spot on his forehead. If you dab paint on a dolphin's forehead, that dolphin will rush to a mirror to see what he looks like. They know who they are.

We infer all the time from the behavior of all sorts of animals that they have selves. They have personalities and wants and desires and the means to seek their satisfaction. Cats and dogs are shoo-ins, but there are some people who even have pet chickens that they claim have distinct personalities. I suppose so. It is hard for an old Iowa farm boy like me to believe that chickens—universally known by people who raise them commercially as the dumbest animals on earth—have any brains at all, but of course they do. If you raise a chicken as a pet, you may be convinced that it is halfway bright and—at least some of the time—self-aware.

This "at least some of the time" goes for human beings too. We are self-conscious a lot less than we think we are. Sometimes when I used to set out to go to the bookstore that was on the route between my house and my office at the university, I found myself arriving at my office, having walked mindlessly past the bookstore. Anyone who has driven a car long distances is familiar with the experience of suddenly realizing that ten miles have gone by and you don't remember a thing about them. We do a lot of things on automatic, just like robots, without thought, and without being aware of doing them. We might be thinking of something else while we blankly carry on with some task, and we often do things without being aware of doing them at all. Sleepwalking is another example of this.

The impossibility of knowing for certain whether or not other people are thinking and have souls derives from the subjectivity of one's mind and thoughts. The only subject who can have your thoughts is you. Just having a thought makes it yours. That is what makes it impossible for you to have someone else's thoughts, or someone else yours. If you have a thought, even if it seems to be an alien thought that comes from somewhere outside you, it is still your thought in your mind. When someone insists that he has someone else's thoughts, or that God is talking to him in his mind, or that someone is communicating with him by telepathy, or that angels have appeared and spoken to him, we don't believe it. We think he is crazy.

But what about Joan of Arc? People thought she was crazy when she was alive, but after her death (by being burned at the stake for heresy) she was canonized as a saint in the Catholic Church. I don't know how the College of Cardinals determined that she really was visited by the Archangel Gabriel.

It is impossible to devise an experiment to determine whether or not the voices people hear (and only they hear) in their heads are from God, but many experiments have been done to determine whether or not some people can read other people's minds (that is, have their thoughts). Great stage shows are put on by mind readers, but their successes can be explained by their ability to guess what people think in certain situations, and their acuteness in guiding people's thoughts. No case of authentic mind reading is known.

In an actual test, suppose you are thinking of a house and the mind reader says you are thinking of a house. Then you think of something else. After a lot of tests, the number of times the mind reader gets it right is no better than would happen if he were just guessing. The same results occur when someone tries to send thoughts to someone else. The number of times the receiver gets it right (many tests have shown) is no better than if the receiver had just guessed.

What about telekinesis? This is the power to move material objects merely by thinking about them. I used to make a professor's bad joke in my classes. I told the students that I could move a material object just by thinking about it. When I had their attention, I raised my arm. Just decide to raise your arm and you can do it. Your decision to raise your arm amounts to your mind willing that your arm rise, and it does. In the same way, you can make a pencil on the table rise in the air simply by reaching out and picking it up.

There is the ancient story that before eating the apple in the Garden of Eden, Adam could make himself have or lose an erection at will. But because he sinned, Adam and all human males thereafter lost control of their erections.

The power we have to move our own bodies is not what is meant by telekinesis. Telekinesis is the process of moving external bodies with thought. You place a pencil on the table in front of you. Then you think hard about the pencil rising. You do not reach out and pick it up, you just concentrate on its rising up from the table and (theoretically) it does. In another example, stage magicians can fake bending a spoon by thought alone, but nobody has ever been able to do it in a controlled experiment. Magicians can do it because human beings can learn to move their fingers faster than people can see. Don't play poker with strangers.

Even scientists can be deceived by people who are very adept and clever at sleight of hand. For example, a few years ago a physicist at Washington University was sure he had found some subjects who could move small objects by thought alone. But he was set up. After he had thoroughly committed himself to the success of the tests, his subjects squealed. They had been trained by Randi, a famous stage magician who has taken as a major task in his life the exposure of frauds. In this instance, he was concerned to show how easy it is to fool trained scientists. Even college students can dupe them. (Anyone who has been a professor for a while ought to have known this already.)

When you get right down to it, even your ability to control your own body by thought is extremely limited. I have always wanted to sit cross-legged and rise right up in the air. So year after year I sat cross-legged on the desk in the front of the classroom and generations of freshman students in my introductory course in philosophy have joined their thoughts with mine to try to get me to levitate. We never succeeded. I sometimes made the students groan by telling them that I can levitate, and then I jump up in the air.

These stories are to remind you that we are in the realm of fantasy here.

Now consider extra-sensory perception. This is the presumed ability to perceive what is happening in places far removed from your body. We do perceive things happening at a distance from us, but that is through the senses. Light waves bounce off mountains to our eyes. Sound waves travel through the air to our ears. This is not what is meant. Extra-sensory perception is supposed to be the perceiving of something without any of our sense organs being stimulated by light waves or anything else coming from that thing.

Suppose one has a dream that one's great aunt was killed in an automobile accident, and lo, that dream happened the same night that one's great aunt was killed in an automobile accident. The dream does not have to happen at exactly the same time she died. Nor do the details have to be just right. Just a hint of them is adequate for many people who have had such dreams to say, "Oh, that's what that strange dream was about," and to believe that they had had extra-sensory perception of such an event.

Again, there is no evidence that people actually have extra-sensory perception of events that are distant in space or time. These claims are hard to test, but the chances of such coordination on the evidence seem to be no more than random. Most people who think they have such experiences, however, do not believe for a moment that they are random. But also they do not keep track of the enormous numbers of dreams and visions and chills that do not have any coordination to any distant events. Also, we are good at making things up. If one improves one's memory of a dream just right (as we all do), one can arrange the dream so that it seems to be about a distant event. Really weird disconnected dreams can then appear to make perfect sense. To make one's dreams fit what really happened, all you have to know is what happened. Then you can fill in the gaps and piece the parts together.

In themselves, dreams, visions, and premonitions are often no different from one's ordinary experiences and thoughts. So even if they were authentic, they would not be much good to one because one can never identify them until one learns through ordinary channels that the event actually occurred. But think of the possibilities if one did have extra-sensory perception, or if one could see ahead a few days or even a few minutes into the future.

The physicist who was duped by Randi the Magician's stooges had received a grant of $500,000 from the will of John McDonnell of McDonnell-Douglas to study extra-sensory perception, telepathy, and telekinesis. One might say that McDonnell was interested in being contacted after he died. Perhaps he didn't want to give up control of the business just because he was dead. On the other hand, consider the business he was in. McDonnell-Douglas was one of the largest manufacturer of warplanes in the world. Now consider that if he had been able to develop telekinesis, he would have had the greatest weapon ever dreamed of by man (it is in fact dreamed of by authors of hundreds of fantasy novels). Instead of having to send a very expensive warplane or missile up in the air to shoot down an enemy plane, you could have someone freeze its controls. Or just stop the heart of the pilot. Think what such a talent would do for assassination. No one would be safe.

But everyone is safe, at least from telekinesis. If anyone had that ability, everyone would know about it. As it happened, McDonnell's $500,000 was not wasted. It was worth testing to see if these powers exist.

If telekinesis and telepathy were possible, these powers would have to be supported by spiritual forces pervading the universe. So far, the only seemingly spiritual forces of which we have any experience fuel our individual abilities to think and move our bodies. These forces extend no farther than our bodies. As for telekinesis and other forms of extra-sensory perception, we are back to the restriction that if you do not somehow have material contact with a material thing, you cannot move it or perceive it.

But one can move one's own body. So if one has the mental power to move one's own body by overcoming the movements determined by natural laws that one's body would otherwise make, then why hasn't the force of will been added to the four forces scientists now recognize in nature? The reason is that the forces of gravity, electromagnetism, and strong and weak nuclear forces are postulated to explain the regular, determined behavior of things in the world. But behavior caused by free will is by definition not regular or determined according to the laws of nature, but is caused solely by one's free will.

The force of free will is meant to explain one's presumed power to interfere with and alter the movements of bodies that are determined by the other four forces. Will power is not conceived of so much as a force, then, but as a counter-force, and an erratic counter-force at that. We can roughly determine its limits (I cannot jump six feet straight up even though I will to), but we cannot define or describe the force of will in terms of regularities such as those covered by natural laws.

A material body always falls the same way in the same circumstances. The law is absolute. But there are no absolute regularities of arm raising, whatever the circumstances. If you sit down, cross your right leg over your left leg, and a doctor taps just below your right knee cap with a little rubber hammer, your right leg will probably jerk upward. A deterministic law can be formulated about that. But whether or not you swing your right leg up and down while you are sitting there waiting is a free choice. You might do it and you might not. That, after all, is what the power of free will is all about. Not just the ability to do something but also the ability not to do something. So no deterministic law can be formulated about leg swinging. Where there are no absolute regularities, there are no grounds for deterministic laws, and thus no cause for postulating a force. This is one reason no force of free will has been unanimously proposed and agreed upon by scientists, but has been for the force of gravity.

Another reason no universal power or force has been postulated to explain free will is the great reluctance of scientists to admit that there are movements in nature undetermined by physical interactions among material things. Statistical laws are OK because they still cover regularities. One can suppose that we do not have 100-percent laws in the statistical cases just because we do not know enough about the situations yet. Presumably if we examined all the factors carefully enough, we could predict with 100-percent accuracy just which patients with syphilis will contract paresis.

Most scientists (some reluctantly) have even accepted the view that some of the behavior of sub-atomic particles is random, thus unlawful, and therefore unpredictable. But they are willing to do this partly because the random behavior of sub-atomic particles averages out to strict determinism among material things above the sub-atomic level. This suggests to some scientists that even on the sub-atomic level there may be hidden factors, which, if ever discerned, will show that movements on the sub-atomic level are also strictly determined. Einstein believed this was true. He said God does not play dice with the universe. (If this is true, then Einstein's God is much more consistent than the God of Moses, Jesus, and Mohammed.)

To understand the difference between a deterministic and an indetermistic world, consider the difference between fantasy and

116

science fiction. In Hal Clement's science fiction novel *Mission of Gravity*, humans explore a planet that has a gravitational force several times that of earth. This makes the mission difficult to carry out, but not impossible. What makes such a novel science fiction is that the author introduces no physically impossible tricks, such as a gravity neutralizer. Everything that takes place must strictly follow natural laws. The described world is deterministic because you can predict what will happen according to those laws.

Fantasy, on the other hand, is freewheeling. It does not conform to strict laws of nature. Some characters have magic powers; others, for no particular reason, do not. Then the hero in need of a certain power sometimes magically acquires it and sometimes does not. There are no consistent laws of nature according to which you can predict what is going to happen. Thus the described world is not lawfully deterministic.

The powers of God, gods, angels, demons, ghosts, and spirits are like those in fantasy. They are erratic, irregular, untrustworthy, and unlawful. The problem with a free force of human will power is that it more befits a realm of fantasy than a realm of science. Free will does not work reliably and regularly, so it follows no absolutely consistent laws. Thus, scientists have not been able to discover laws of human behavior under the influence of the force of free will as they have for the behavior of material bodies under the influence of the force of gravity. Without deterministic laws, there is no reason to postulate a force of free will as an explanation or cause of one's ability to move one's own body. This ability, then, remains not only unexplained, but also suspect. The feeling that one has free will and makes free choices and thus determines some of one's own behavior may simply accompany one's fully determined behavior. Our sense of making a choice may be part of what is determined, while the choice itself is not in any way the cause of what happens. The philosophical term for this is supervenience. The sense of making a choice supervenes on, but does not influence, one's behavior.

But suppose that one's free choices did in fact always accurately precede one's behavior. Then it would seem that one's choices cause this behavior. Fine. Even so, according to Hume, this makes the force of free will no more a real cause than any other force. Remember that

Hume's analysis of physical causation is that it is nothing more than regular sequences of one thing following another. That is, according to Hume, one's sense that one freely chooses is misleading. It merely precedes, or accompanies, what one's body does.

The powers of the human mind are truly spectacular. Telepathy and telekinesis are fantasies, but one can cause oneself to have apparently mystical experiences. The easiest way for one to get into oceanic contact with the infinite is by popping pills or by eating hallucinogenic mushrooms, but I don't advise doing that. The problem is that when one takes LSD or sniffs coke, it is like throwing a hand grenade into one's brain. You may get the effects you want, but sometimes the wrong synapses are activated and you can have a very bad trip. Even on good trips, these drugs disrupt your brain a lot more than is required to feel good. It is much better to learn how to get these effects without ingesting any foreign materials that bomb your brain.

Suppose you want to feel at one with the universe. Meditation is the ancient tried and true way to have such a mystical experience. I am not going to describe how to go about it. You can find instructions in many other books. I just want to assure you that it works. What more is there to say about it than that? It works.

As it turns out, there is a lot more to be said that is pertinent to our interests in this book. Consider these techniques: meditation, but also fasting, isolation, sensory deprivation, exposure to extremes of heat or cold, chanting or dancing or drumming until you drop, even self-flagellation and torture (although here we are getting into the harmful realm of bombing the body as drugs bomb the brain). Do these techniques transport your mind or soul into a realm that is truly beyond the bodily realm of material things? This is certainly what mystics, religious ecstatics, and many ordinary meditators think. (Other meditators think it is just a healthy way to relax and to relieve the tensions of daily life, but perhaps they are just unimaginative.)

The mystical or global or oceanic experience is one in which the self seems to fall away, time slows or stops, and the personal boundaries that ordinarily separate one's individuality from the rest of the universe dissolve. In other words, there is a feeling of expanding outward into the infinite universe. Most particularly, one loses one's sense of one's body. Thus the feeling of separation from the rest of the material world disappears. Sometimes there is a sense of floating, or of swift movement up and away from the world.

Again, skeptics should be assured that this experience really happens. Furthermore, it does not harm your brain the way popping pills does. Or drinking alcohol. Or smoking tobacco, crack, or dope.

The question is: Does this unworldly experience show that the soul is truly separate from the body and can be liberated from it? Consider the fact that meditative techniques—as well as some physical or mental shocks—can sometimes lead to out-of-body experiences, in which you seem to float above your body and look down on it.

To start, let's not worry for the moment about *how* the mind does it, but instead focus on *what* the mind does. Neurophysiologists such as Andrew Newberg at the University of Pennsylvania have scanned the brains of meditating Tibetan Buddhists and Franciscan nuns to discover that in deep meditation there is a damping down of the part of the brain that orients a person in space and provides the body image that separates one from the outer physical world. Also, the activity of the part of the brain that is always active when one is alert and self-conscious is slowed greatly.

This dissolving of boundaries of one's body and self is never complete. Otherwise, one could not have and remember these experiences. But the curtain between one's self and the rest of the universe is, or at least seems to be, drawn back. It is no wonder, then, that such global experiences are often interpreted in terms of religious revelation. Some people think they see God. Others think they have had a premonition of Paradise. Many believe that at least for the moment they were merged with or in tune with the universe or understood what it all means.

The brain activity associated with these experiences seems to be the same in all cultures, but the specific content of the experiences varies from culture to culture. Buddhist monks do not see crosses or feel the presence of Jesus as Christian mystics do. But the basic experiences, and particularly the brain activity, are the same in all cultures.

No one disputes the existence of these experiences. No one should doubt that they follow from changes in brain activity caused by drugs or by meditation. The correlation of these experiences with certain brain activity is well confirmed. But to prove the independence of the mind or soul, we have to show that such experiences can occur apart from the brain. Materialists argue that the correlation shows that such experiences are merely the result of that brain activity. Mystical experiences are just unusual effects of neuronal firings that anyone can have. The easy and dangerous way to generate such ecstatic experiences is to take drugs. Alcohol alters one's consciousness in a usually mild and generally pleasant way—as most of the human beings on this planet know. Marijuana does too. But many mind-altering drugs are addicting and definitely do not transport one to Heaven.

The drug connection in particular provides a strong argument that such experiences are simply brain-generated and brain-confined. That they are pretty weird and lead some people to think they have encountered the infinite or God is just an illusory side effect of chemical and neurological activity in the brain. Materialists conclude that what is really real is the brain activity. The mental effects are both illusory and inconsequential, that is, they mean nothing and play no role in the causal chain of brain activity. The answer to that is that we all know that our thoughts do have consequences. These mental experiences have profound effects on people's lives. The problem is that we cannot conceive how one's mental thoughts could act on one's material body.

Mystical experiences are very powerful. What I focus on here is the view that the mind does have the ability, all by itself, to cause one to have out-of-the-world experiences, and they are very impressive. We can reach them through meditation.

So assume that the mind has the power to control brain activity. This assumption is so commonplace and automatic that we take a great amount of our controlling activity for granted. For example, I concentrate to keep my mind on the subject of this book, to put ideas and sentences together clearly and coherently. To do so, I block out many of the messages coming through my nerves to the brain. I make an effort to ignore noise, thirst, discomfort, peripheral vision, and the cat. I retreat into myself to get the job done. I push the outer world aside.

I have explored a lot of caves. Sometimes after a cave trip, I find large bruises and cuts on my arms and legs that I had gotten by crawling and climbing through tight spots. But I had been so intent on what I was doing that I had not felt the bumps and abrasions at the time, and afterward I could not remember how I got them.

People at the symphony sometimes lose themselves in the music. Just ordinary concentration requires one to take control of one's brain to damp down some of its activity. One learns to ignore a lot of the sensory information that is coming in. On a much grander scale, the ability to do this damping leads some people to global, or, if you will, mystical experiences.

You can learn to relax. You can also learn to control your heartbeat and your body temperature. These are not easy to learn, but the human mind can do it. You can improve your golf game by playing mind games. Many top athletes utilize the power the mind has to calm and focus the body. Any klutz can hit a golf ball. Training in the mental techniques of Zen will help you smooth your swing.

How do we do it? I am reminded of a story of how the physicist Richard Feynman solved incredibly difficult problems in mathematics. Feynman would look for a moment at a problem scrawled across half the blackboard. He would put his fists on his forehead and screw up his face in a tortured expression for a few moments. Then he would smile and give the answer. The story continues, of course, that it would take an ordinary physicist hours to solve the problem—to discover that Feynman was right.

The impressive thing here is that ordinary physicists have the will power to concentrate on the problem for half a day, and to control the attention of their minds to work the problem out. Not many people are geniuses, but most of us do have the ability to get our mental ducks in line.

The brain is the machine of thought. It is tempting to say that Feynman was simply blessed with a powerful computer of a brain. That may be so, but Feynman was the one who posed the problem to that brain and set it to work. This is the premise we are operating under at present: that the mind has the power to move the body, which means the power to control the brain. Most movements of the body derive from nerve impulses that originate in the brain. Brain movements that cause intentional body movements (such as raising one's arm) originate from our mind's capacity to control the nerve impulses sent out from the brain. *If* there is a mind separate from and independent of the brain, then it has immense powers for controlling the brain.

Don't get lost. The subject of investigation here is the existence and powers of the mind as the soul.

We have come to the impasse again. If mind and brain are distinct and separate entities, and if the mind has (some) control of the brain, how does the mind do it? What is the force or power that the mind exerts on the brain? How is this force deployed? How does mentality move the material brain?

The same questions can be asked in reverse. How does a material body act on a mind? I have remarked that when Princess Elisabeth asked Descartes how mind and body interact, he could not give an intelligible answer. It happens because God makes it so, he said. That answer may be good enough for pious Christians. In fact, it was not good enough for Princess Elisabeth, and certainly it is not good enough for twenty-first-century neuroscientists and philosophers. We don't know how the mind acts on the brain. In fact, we don't even know for sure that the mind does act on the brain, however much it appears that it does.

The apparent powers of the mind are immense. The problem is that if they exist, they are outside the realm of natural science. If an immaterial mind or soul exists, it is outside the realm of material things. The soul has always been considered to be in the realm of the supernatural. Scientists simply cannot abide the mind also being in the realm of the supernatural. The move to identify the mind with the brain is in some large part motivated by the desire to bring the mind into the realm of science. The brain is a material body that operates according to natural laws, just as does any other material body. Consequently, if the mind is the brain, the mind also must operate according to natural laws. But the mind sure does not seem to be law-abiding. What materialists must do, then, is show how the apparently supernatural and erratic operations of free will are actually natural and law-abiding. This is what philosophers mean who say they are working on the problem of naturalizing the mind.

If the mind is a natural, law-abiding entity, however, then how can it have free will in the freewheeling sense that we all ordinarily understand it? And if it is not free in that sense, how can we have any control over our destinies? Would not everything we do and think, down to the last tiny thought and bodily motion, be determined? Here we are again at the problem of free will in a physically deterministic universe.

Remember that even if there is randomness and chance in the sub-atomic levels of the physical universe, this would not solve the problem of providing us with free will. I mention above that on atomic levels and above, the sub-atomic realm of chance evens out into deterministic, lawful behavior. But even if there were random chance behavior on the level of bodies the size of our own, such chance and randomness would not save free will. It would be as unsatisfactory for our free choices to be generated at random and by chance, as it would be if they were fully determined by the laws of nature. We don't want our choices to be either random or strictly determined. What we want and mean by free will is that each of us makes the choices and freely determines the behavior of our bodies according to our interests and desires. For this to take place, the force of free will must be a power that cannot be explained by the deterministic laws of nature.

Chapter 6.
The Mind and the Brain

The average human brain weighs about three pounds and consists of a hundred billion neurons interconnected with one another by ten trillion synapses. The brain itself is part of the human body's central nervous system with connections all over the body. A good short introduction to the structure and operations of the brain is "Brain Events" by Brian Cooney, pp. 53–73 in *The Place of the Mind* that he edited. I quote from that article below.

What is important for our purposes is that the number of possible neuronal connections in the brain (not to mention in the entire nervous system) is in the billions of trillions. If you consider the brain as a computer, this complexity is adequate for the encoding and manipulating of millions of times as many mental experiences and operations as occur in a human lifetime. If the brain is the mind, the overkill factor is out of this world.

Not just the number of potential operations, but also the scope and analytic strength of the mind-brain is barely touched by the average person. What is surprising is not that there are geniuses such as Descartes, Newton, and Einstein. What is surprising is that there are not more such geniuses. In fact, no genius, not even Richard Feynman, has ever managed to compute problems of the complexity the brain is theoretically capable of handling, but the potential is there.

Pharmacologists continue to try to find drugs that enhance brain (and thus mental) activity. Nicotine is one such drug. It helps the mind concentrate. Many people smoke to reduce nervous tension. Amphetamines are not called speed for nothing. The French existentialist philosopher Jean-Paul Sartre wrote some of his very influential books while he was on amphetamines. So far, however, no mind-enhancing drugs have been found that are not both addictive and harmful. For relaxing and concentrating, Zen techniques and meditation work as well as drugs.

Our beginning point continues to be the belief of most people that the mind or soul is an immaterial entity separate and distinct from the material brain. This is the main hope for immortality when the brain dies. One's mind obviously uses the brain to sense things, to reason, to remember, and to imagine, perhaps by operating it as a computer. The mind also apparently has free will to use the brain to override and change bodily movements determined by the natural laws of physics. But it is impossible for an immaterial mind to do these things. An immaterial mind has no way to act on or influence a material brain.

The only conclusion is that the mind is not immaterial, but rather is some aspect of the material brain. Thus we have to figure out how the brain can control both its operations that generate thought, and those that control body movements. Why do we have to explain these things? Because we know they happen.

What is it about the brain that makes it the mind? The mind arises out of the multiple trillions of complex electrochemical interactions that take place in the brain. The evidence for this is that when the brain dies and all that neuronal activity stops, the mind disappears. When the neurons are inactive, when all of them stop firing, when the curve on the monitor screen goes flat, the mind-brain is dead. This is a major reason why neurophysiologists think the brain is the mind.

The living brain is a hive of electrochemical activity among the neurons. Complex changing patterns are formed by these electrochemical interactions. The mind is not merely the interacting material neurons, but is essentially the dynamic changing patterns of their interrelations. Again, a dead, inactive brain is not the mind.

The mind, then, is the incredibly complex pattern of dynamic interrelations among the neuronal firings of the living material brain. The pattern itself is something other than the firing neurons. If this dynamic pattern could lift itself out of the brain to have a being of its own, it might serve as an immaterial mind or soul that exists separate from the brain. Alas, it is not possible for a set of relations to exist independently. To exist, relations must always be manifested in something. The patterned mind in action, then, is manifested in and depends on the brain for its existence. In itself, it is just an abstract pattern that cannot exist by itself alone. The pattern can, of course, be conceived of independently of the brain. For example, you might imagine something other than the brain—say a computer made of silicon chips—that exhibits the same pattern of relations.

This must be stressed: One can consider the dynamic pattern of the mind without thinking of what exhibits the pattern (neurons, chips), but the pattern cannot exist by itself. Any existing pattern must always exist as the pattern of something such as neurons or chips. Thus the mind or soul as a set of interacting relationships among neurons must be manifested in the material of the brain. The conclusion from this would seem to have to be that the soul—as a set of relations—cannot exist independently of a brain.

Consciousness appears when neurons in the brain fire in a wave pattern of 40 Hertz per second. The mind consisting of the neuronal activity of the brain is active, however, even when neurons are not firing in the 40-Hertz range. Thus there is a lot of unconscious brain or mind activity. This goes against Descartes's belief that the mind must be self-consciously thinking to exist ("I think, therefore I am"). It is supported by Freud's insights about unconscious fears and desires, and by many neurological studies that show complex brain activity even when people are not self-conscious. You know from your own experience that unconscious brain activity takes place. Sometimes you go to bed at night with a problem in mind, and in the morning you wake up with the answer. No conscious thinking occurred while you were asleep. Or you remember something you did not notice at the time it happened. Or when asked why you are behaving like a moron, it suddenly occurs to you that it is because you are in love. A lot more of our personality traits and beliefs are generated and stored in our brains unconsciously than we might want to admit.

In sum, a set of relations cannot exist by itself. For a set of relations to exist, it must be exemplified or exhibited by existing things that are related to one another in that particular way. What I am suggesting is that the mind consists of the changing patterns of dynamic relations that are exhibited by the electrochemical activity of the neurons that make up the brain. The mind is not the neurons themselves, but the patterns manifested by the firing neurons.

For there to be a mind, then, there must be a living active brain. What distinguishes each living active brain from all the others is the distinctive set of relationships among the trillions of electrochemical interactions taking place among the neurons of that brain. We know that the pattern itself cannot actually be separated from the neurons and the rate at which they fire, but we can think of the pattern separately. So here is a crucial question: Could the pattern take on a life of its own and somehow gain the power to guide its own development? I don't mean: *Could* it exist independently? Because it could not. I mean: Could this materially manifested pattern impose variations of itself back on the material parts of the brain to control the pattern of firings of neurons in the brain? If it could, then perhaps it could interrupt the deterministic chain of material events that cause bodily motions, and substitute other bodily motions. This is just what is required if the mind is to have free will.

Self-control by the brain-mind is not an entirely outlandish suggestion. Consider a simple machine with a flywheel. A flywheel is a device designed to keep a machine always running at the same speed. One variety of flywheel works by having hinged arms with weights on their ends. When the machine is running at the proper speed, the flywheel goes around with the arms folded in. But when the machine speeds up faster than desired, the arms fly out to make the machine work harder to turn the flywheel, and this slows the machine. When the proper speed is reached, the flywheel arms fold back down again. The machine with a flywheel is thus programmed to operate at a given uniform speed.

This example suggests that the brain might be controlled by a modulated pattern of neuron firings. Could a program have the capacity to operate the brain computer? No. As explained above, a program in itself could never do anything. It is just another abstract set of relations that cannot exist by itself. A program has to be embodied in a computer, which computer in turn must be operated by someone, just as someone has to turn a machine with a flywheel on and off. What is required for a self-operated brain is that the pattern of neuron firings must impose itself back onto the brain not just to modulate, but also to generate new patterns of neuron firing in the brain. The living brain would then be something like a self-operating computer.

But even if a *pattern* of firing taking did take over and impose new patterns of firing on the neurons, would this constitute free will? Would the mind-brain be altering and controlling its own operations? Would it be exhibiting free will? Or would the new patterns be imposed on the brain not by choice, but rather be determined by the previous firings of the neurons, as all other sequences of material change are determined by the material events that have gone before?

We have come to the crux of the matter. Let's go slowly now to see what we need. Consider the brains of slugs and worms. These brains have very few neurons, probably not enough to generate minds. These brains control all the behavior of slugs and worms. Their behavior is reflexive and instinctive, that is, without thought. Slugs and worms are hardwired. Humans, however, have thinking minds. They innovate and invent new ways to behave in new (and even in old) situations. A lot of human behavior is reflexive and instinctive, but not (we assume) all human behavior is hardwired. How do we explain the deviations from determined behavior?

What do human beings want? (The theological version of this question is: What are we here for?) Most human beings want to survive, reproduce, and live a good life—in that order. These goals are end results of an evolutionary process that began with the first simple self-replicating structures that fell together after the Big Bang. Self-replicators evolved from inorganic to simple and then to more complex life forms. In the course of this evolution, brains were developed to monitor and control the behavior of animal bodies. Human beings are very complex life forms with highly developed brains. Those brains operate to further the reproduction, survival, and good lives of you and me.

Note well: Although this exposition is in standard evolutionary biological terminology, it could as well be offered as an exposition of the world as God created it.

What is the mind for? The human mind—its self-conscious sensing, reasoning, remembering, and imagining—helps the human organism to survive. Descartes and Locke said that sensing colors, sounds, touches, odors, and tastes, plus pains and bodily feelings, helps us respond quickly to situations in the outer world. Consider the fact, for example, that the human body is made up of about three trillion cells (and each cell is made up of many atoms, each of which is made up of multiple sub-atomic particles). If one *perceived* material bodies as interacting collections of atoms (not to mention sub-atomic particles), the result would be (as Descartes and Locke realized) so complex that one could never integrate and understand what one is perceiving. Think of the computations that would be required to figure out where to move to hit a tennis ball. But if one perceives gross collections of atoms as a tennis ball, the court, and the net, then one can move quickly to the right spot.

The thoughts and sensations one is conscious of are manifestations of millions, billions, and trillions of microsecond neuronal interactions in our brains. One cannot pay attention to them all, but one can pay attention to gross representations (one's sensations and thoughts) of some of them. The very slow activities of sensing and reasoning make possible our comprehension of what the immensely rapid activity of neurons in one's brain and nervous system represent in the world outside one's brain.

Here, in a long quotation from Brian Cooney about sensory encoding in the brain, is how information about the outer world gets to our brains. I know it is dense, but bear down. You want to know about the mind and soul. So read this. The example is the eye:

> What the retina does with light is remarkable not merely for the fact that it converts light into neural impulses, but even more because it faithfully translates into the language of impulses the dimensions of so many properties of the light stimulus. I will refer to this aspect of transduction [the conversion from one form of energy (electrical, chemical, mechanical) to another] as **encoding**. We have already seen how the working of the center-surround receptive fields encodes boundaries of contrasting illumination. Color is another good example of encoding. At any site along the retinal surface there are populations of the three kinds of cones, each kind firing more often as the light it absorbs

approaches its preferred frequency (corresponding to blue or yellow or red). These cones synapse [connect] with types of ganglion cells that also differ in their preferred frequencies. Each of these ganglion cells has an axon that bundles with the others leading away from that site, ultimately joining millions more to form the optic nerve going to the brain. Within the bundle from a particular site impulses will be occurring with different frequencies in different fibers, and this spatiotemporal pattern of impulses in the bundle encodes with great precision the color of the light absorbed at that site. Furthermore, the *locus* of the light source in the visual field is encoded in the locus of stimulation on the retina, and this locus in turn is encoded in the segregation of fibers in the optic nerve, and then by the termination of those fibers at a particular spot on the sheet of brain neurons that receives visual input. The original retinal locus is in the receptive field for that spot in the brain tissue.

The auditory system provides us with another striking example of transduction and encoding. . . . A sound composed of many frequencies, such as a musical chord, will produce waves with peaks at different sites along the basilar membrane [of the ear]. Thus the chord is transduced and encoded as a set of impulses simultaneously traveling along frequency-specific fibers from these different sites and terminating at corresponding sites on sheets of neurons in the auditory zone of the cerebral cortex [in the brain].

It isn't just the variables *within* one modality (such as different colors in vision or different frequencies of sounds) that are encoded in the patterns of impulses moving along bundles of fibers to specific sites in the brain. The same code also renders what we experience as the qualitative difference between color and sound, or between heat and pain. In these cases there are separate cables (nerves) and brain terminal sites for what is otherwise the same sort of content: patterned impulses. This neural code can be exhaustively analyzed in the mathematical language of spatial relations, energy, duration, frequency, and so on. (Cooney, "Brain Events," pp. 64–65)

130

In other words, the sensory system maps the external world in the brain.

All of this minute data is utilized by one's brain to provide gross sensory representations (images) of the vast collections of atoms and sub-atomic particles that make up the material bodies in the world that one is conscious of.

Do these bodies really exist in the outer world as one perceives them? No. They exist there as collections of atoms that cause us to see them as bodies, including our own bodies. But nothing like the sensory representations of these bodies actually exists outside our minds. It is just that a collection of atoms looks like a body to us. This bothers some philosophers a great deal. Because what one sees is not like what is out there, Descartes worried that there might not be an outside world at all. Perhaps a demon causes our minds to have perceptions of bodies, and all that exists is the demon and our minds. Not to worry, because today we have scientific techniques for inferring the existence of atoms and sub-atomic particles. But the demon could cause the perceptions from which we infer that too. Well . . . let's assume that those atoms and subatomic particles (or matter and energy) are really out there and cause us to have representations of bodies, and that this has come about through evolution because it helps us survive.

But Descartes is right that our scientific techniques do not make it absolutely certain that there are atoms outside our minds. Nothing is absolutely certain except that when you are self-consciously thinking you know you are existing. You could worry about this lack of certainty if you got into a serious metaphysical or theological funk. What if there is nothing in the world but me causing myself to have sensations (solipsism, i.e., only I exist)? What if there is no God (atheism)? Most people enjoy thinking about such questions, but don't really take them seriously. That is, most people never really doubt either that there is a world like the one that one perceives, or that God exists. Are they absolutely certain about this? Most of them say they are, even though the rise of modern science in the seventeenth century resulted in some part from giving up the search for absolute certainty and concentrating on the development of probabilistic physics. The success of science is the strongest argument for the existence of an external world of atoms, neurons, and sub-atomic particles. But of course that they exist is not absolutely certain. But, again, never mind. Let's get on with what we think we know.

Our perceptual transformation of the rapidly moving atoms into images of bodies helps us get about in the world. To get about in the world to satisfy our needs and desires, it would be of great advantage for us to have free will. We assume that we do have free will. Then the best guess as to how the human brain exerts discretionary—free choice—control over the human body is that the patterns of neural brain activity can modulate and alter themselves. How?

One answer is that brain activity is like the weather. Tiny differences in a complex system cause vastly different results. The difficulty in predicting the weather is not that it is undetermined, but that such a vast number of tiny differences can result in such greatly different results. The same is the case in brain activity. Such systems are modeled mathematically with what is called chaos theory, which is an unfortunate name because chaos suggests chance and lack of determinism. In fact there is no chance involved and these systems are strictly deterministic. They are just so vast and complex that it is difficult, if not humanly impossible, for us to figure them out, so they appear to be developing indeterministically by chance. The neurons in the brain constitute such a system.

I point out above that the notion that we have free will to choose our actions implies that we have the power to alter the patterns of neuronal firing in our brains to bring about thoughts and images of our choosing, and also to move our bodies as we please.

Descartes said that the way free will acts is by altering the movements of the pineal gland in the brain, which he thought was the central receiving organ for all reports from the senses. He said that the pineal gland automatically responds to sensory reports with instinctual responses. But Descartes also believed that the mind can overcome the automatic responses dictated by the pineal gland, so that the pineal gland sends out messages in the form of vibrations of nerves to the muscles to move the body the way the mind wants.

The contemporary hypothesis of neuronal activity is similar to Descartes's except that there is no immaterial mind making the choices. Instead, there is the complex pattern of neuronal firings in the brain. What is proposed is that the body's sensory system has evolved to provide gross, bodily images of the various groupings of the zillions of atoms in the world. We see chairs and human bodies, and not the atoms of which they are made. It furthers the survival of our own bodies to reason about the gross bodies. We seem to have the power to control our bodies by making small alterations in the brain's automatic responses to sensory inputs. These alterations result in bodily movements different from those that would have resulted if the mind had not intervened. Once again, one's belief that one has free will implies that the deterministic behavior of the brain can be overridden and superseded by the free choice of the mind.

The major objection to this theory of the mind's interference with the physically determined behavior of the brain and the body is that it requires overriding the physical laws of nature. This bothered Descartes, who suggested that bodily motions are not overcome, but merely redirected. Newton pointed out that redirection itself requires the expenditure of new physical energy, but an immaterial mind has no physical energy to expend. Human bodies, though, take in energy in the form of food and use this energy to maintain themselves. It would make sense for us to have free will, the self-conscious ability to control neuronal activity to alter bodily movements to facilitate our survival. The exercise of free choice would not require much energy. Very small changes in the patterns of neuronal firings can result in major changes in muscle movements of the body. As Cooney reports,

> We go from micro- to macro-dimensions in the transition from the [small amounts of] electrochemical energy expended in the molecular [neural] events preceding muscle contraction to the [large amounts of] mechanical energy in the contraction itself. (p. 62).

We don't have to know consciously which patterns to change. If we do have free will, the connections between our willing and the pattern changes have developed in us through mutations and trial and error during the course of evolution. (Or, God made us that way.) Everything we do requires this micro-neuronal to macro-muscular movement of our bodies.

The self-conscious mind, then, is for self-regulation aimed ultimately at self-replication. That's how the world as we know it began,
and that is how it is now. The mind is a high-level, self-replicating
machine. Its goal is to reproduce. Dawkins argues for this in his book
The Selfish Gene. But if that is all we are for, you might ask, how
does it come about that humans have developed so elaborately that
they write books like this one? The answer is that the development of
science and the spread of knowledge help the human species to survive.

One sign of a good theory is that it answers questions you didn't
ask. The theory that the mind is the continuously active neuronal firings in a living brain could explain why so much of one's thinking
consists of sudden insights. Often one reasons consciously step-by-
step, as when one adds a column of figures. But many times one bears
down and nothing happens until all at once the answer pops into
one's head. We bear down the way Richard Feynman solved difficult
math problems. It is not new to say that your mind or brain was
working unconsciously, but the theory that the mind consists of continuously active neuronal firings operating in patterns that represent
the things you are thinking about explains how you got the answer.
The steps in reasoning were unconscious, but the answer becomes
conscious. The goal you set, anyway, was the answer, not the steps of
reasoning or how you got it. If you want to know those steps, you
can concentrate on them, and they will come to consciousness too.

But come on, you say, do we really have free will? If the body is
part of the deterministic material world—and it is—then even the little alterations made by free will have to be determined. So we're not
free after all.

Spinoza said that the more you know how you are determined,
the freer you are. I have presented a contemporary deterministic theory of what you are that explains what he means. When it comes
right down to it, you are your body. You are your brain. You are your
mind, which consists of patterns of neuronal firings in your brain.
You seem to have the free-will power to adjust those neuronal patterns to cause the alteration of your thoughts and of the movements
of your body that were initially determined from outside.

But in fact, according to Brian Cooney in *The Place of the Mind* and Benjamin Libet in *Mind Time*, the brain activity that causes the alterations of one's thoughts and of the movements of one's body occurs a microsecond before you are conscious of your decision. So your apparently free decisions are themselves determined. *But*, and here is the crucial point, it is still you—your brain—that makes that determination. You experience this determination as the making of a free choice. The bottom line is that even if your choices are determined, it is still *you* determining them.

But is there really no immaterial, immortal soul?

There just seems to be no way there could be. Even if there were, it wouldn't be *you*. To be you, your mind-soul would have to be installed in a human body. Again, at least Judeo-Christian-Muslim theologians have long known this. That's why the doctrine of the Resurrection is in the Bible. And so I conclude this investigation with an up-to-the-minute contemporary scientific explanation for the necessity of the Christian doctrine of the Rapture. Only if there is a miraculous restoration of our bodies at the end of time will our souls survive death.

EPILOGUE

In sum, both the argument for and the argument against the existence of God derive from the rational conclusion that the concept of God is contradictory, and thus unintelligible.

Non-believers present this to argue that the religions deriving from the Bible are meaningless, just as the notion of a square circle is contradictory and thus makes no sense. Believers glory in the mystery of God.

The basic arguments for and against God's existence are as follows:

An omnipotent, omniscient, omni-good, etc. God
1. created the universe and everything in it including Himself out of nothing, but this is impossible for neither can something come from nothing nor can something cause itself,
2. but given that God is the Creator of everything, God is thus the cause of everything that takes place in the universe, except that
3. because God gives human beings free will—which is logically impossible given that God is the cause of everything—but given that humans have free will, God is not responsible for human choices and actions, in particular
4. God is not responsible for Adam's disobedience, on the basis of which God cursed all humankind who have henceforth been born in sin, and also even though God makes it impossible for humans not to sin, God is not responsible for human sins,
5. nor does God cause evil, which seems to go against the claim that God causes everything and also seems to be unfair given that, after all, God caused Adam and humankind to sin and do evil, which leads to the conclusion that this God is hidden and ineffable, and supernatural—that God is inscrutable and cannot be understood through reason but only by faith.

Believers in the religions of the book (Old Testament, New Testament, the Koran, and the Book of Mormon) must believe in all the above and also that

6. God is both one and three persons: Father, Son, and Holy Ghost,

7. Jesus Christ is both human and divine, was immaculately conceived and born of a virgin, and

8. numerous other miracles, preeminently that of the Eucharist, that bread and wine are turned into immense quantities of Christ's flesh and blood.

A particularly difficult item of Christian doctrine that derives from (1), that God created everything, is

9. the doctrine of Predestination: that even prior to God's creation of the universe, every human being's salvation or damnation is predetermined by God. But

10. on the basis of (2), God's giving human beings free will, one should be able to earn salvation through worship and good works, but again on the basis of (1), God's creating and causing everything, we cannot through our human efforts earn salvation.

11. God gives us Grace, gratuitously and without any merit on our part, so we can overcome our inborn tendency to sin, but

12. this leads to further incomprehensibilities, because the good actions made possible only by God's Grace are without credit toward earning salvation, and in fact,

13. all of one's actions, perpetrated with or without the help of God's grace, are irrelevant to salvation or damnation, because (full circle) God predetermines the saved and the damned with no consideration given to human actions, which makes sense given (1), that God creates and causes everything, except that the whole story is an enigma because God caused us all to sin in the first place.

This exposition of Christian doctrine as contradictory and

unintelligible is why many people who depend on reason and not on faith are atheists.

But . . .

A few years ago I published an article titled "Descartes Knows Nothing." In it I argue that the three ideas that Descartes claims God puts in our minds at birth—of mind, matter, and God—are empty of meaning, and thus that Descartes knows nothing of mind, matter, or God. As for God, Descartes says that it is beyond the capacity of the human intellect to understand God (or, as above, the concept of God) on grounds of reason, so Descartes accepts God's existence on faith.

In response to this article, an old friend, Jean-Luc Marion, who is a devout Christian and a brilliant scholar, said to me,

"Red! I always knew you were a believer! You are exactly right! God is ineffable! We can only believe in Him by faith!"

BIBLIOGRAPHY

From one viewpoint this bibliography is greatly inflated, but from another it is drastically incomplete. It is in fact a compromise. It contains enough to get you started on most of the subjects covered in this book. After that, you're on our own.

Alston, William P. "Christian Experience and Christian Belief," in Alvin Plantinga & Nicholas Wolterstorff, editors, *Faith and Rationality: Reason and Belief in God*. Notre Dame: University of Notre Dame Press, 1983.

Aquinas, Thomas. *Of God and His Creatures (Summa contra gentiles)*. London: Burns & Oates, 1905.

Aristotle. *Basic Works*. New York: Random House, 1941.

Armour, Leslie. *"Infini Rien." Pascal's Wager and the Human Paradox*. Carbondale: Southern Illinois University Press, 1993.

Armstrong, David M. *The Mind-Body Problem: An Opinionated Introduction*. Boulder: Westview Press, 1999.

Augustine, Saint. *Confessions*, translated by R. S. Pine-Coffin, Harmondsworth: Penguin Books, 1961.

———. *On Free Choice of the Will*. Indianapolis: Hackett, 1993.

———. *The Problem of Free Choice*. New York. Newman Press, 1955.

Ayer, Alfred Jules. *Language, Truth and Logic*. London: Victor Gollancz, 1936.

Bering, Jesse M. "The Cognitive Psychology of Belief in the Supernatural." *American Scientist*, Vol. 94, 2006, pp. 142–49.

Berkeley, George. *Three Dialogues Between Hylas and Philonous*. La Salle: Open Court, 1955.

Boyer, Pascal. *Religion Explained: The Evolutionary Origins of Religious Thought*. New York: Basic Books, 2001.

Calvin, John. *Concerning the Eternal Predestination of God.* London: James Clark, 1961.

Carraud, Vincent. "Pascal's Anti-Augustinianism," *Perspectives on Science*, Vol. 15, 2007, pp. 450–92.

Cashmore, Anthony R. "The Lucretian Swerve: The Biological Basis of Human Behavior and the Criminal Justice System," *PNAS*, 9 March 2010, Vol. 107, pp. 4499–4504.

Chalmers, David J. *The Conscious Mind: In Search of a Fundamental Theory.* New York: Oxford University Press, 1996.

Churchland, Paul M. *Matter and Consciousness: A Contemporary Introduction to the Philosophy of Mind.* Cambridge: MIT Press, 1988.

Collins, James. *God in Modern Philosophy.* London: Routledge & Kegan Paul, 1960.

Cooney, Brian (editor). *The Place of the Mind.* Belmont: Wadsworth, 2000, "Brain Events," pp. 64–65.

Copleston, F. C. *Aquinas.* Harmondsworth: Penguin Books, 1955.

Dakin, A. *Calvinism.* Port Washington: Kennikat Press, 1940.

Dawkins, Richard. *The God Delusion.* New York: Houghton Mifflin, 2006.

Dennett, Daniel C. *Breaking the Spell: Religion as a Natural Phenomenon.* New York: Viking, 2006.

Descartes, René. *Œuvres complètes*, ed. by Charles Adam and Paul Tannery, 11 vols., Paris: J. Vrin, 1964–1974.

———. *The Philosophical Writings of Descartes*, Vols. 1 & 2, translated by John Cottingham, Robert Stoothoff, and Dugald Murdoch; Vol. 3, translated by John Cottingham, Robert Stoothoff, Dugald Murdoch, and Anthony Kenny. Cambridge: Cambridge University Press, Vol. 1, 1985; Vol. 2, 1984; Vol. 3, 1991.

———. *Meditations on First Philosophy* (1641). Cambridge: Cambridge University Press, 1986.

Drake, Durant. *Problems of Religion: An Introductory Survey.* New York: Greenwood Press, 1986.

Eagleton, Terry. *Reason, Faith, and Revolution: Reflections on the God Debate*. New Haven: Yale University Press, 2009.

Erasmus, Desiderius and Martin Luther. *Discourse on Free Will*. Translated and edited by Ernst F. Winter. New York: Frederick Unger Publishing Company, 1961.

Feser, Edward. *The Last Superstition: A Refutation of the New Atheism*. South Bend: St. Augustine's Press, 2008.

Freud, Sigmund. *Totem and Taboo*. New York: W. W. Norton, 1950.

Godwin, Malcolm. *Angels: An Endangered Species*. New York: Simon and Schuster, 1990.

Goldmann, Lucien. *The Hidden God*. London: Routledge & Kegan Paul, 1964.

Goodall, Jane. *Reasons for Hope: A Spiritual Journey*. New York: Warner Books, 1999.

Goodenough, Ursula. *The Sacred Depths of Nature*. New York: Oxford University Press, 1998.

Gould, Stephen Jay. *Rocks of Ages: Science and Religion in the Fullness of Life*. New York: Ballantine Books, 1999.

Gregory of Nyssa. *On the Soul and Resurrection*. Crestwood: St. Vladimir's Seminary Press, 1993.

Harris, Sam. *The End of Faith: Religion, Terror, and the Future of Reason*. New York: W. W. Norton, 2004.

———. *Letter to a Christian Nation*. New York: Alfred A. Knopf, 2006.

Hawking, Stephen W. *The Theory of Everything: The Origin and Fate of the Universe*. New York: New Millennium Press, 2002.

Hedges, Chris. *I Don't Believe in Atheists*. New York: Free Press, 2008.

Hegel, Georg Wilhelm Friedrich. *Phenomenology of Spirit*. Oxford: Oxford University Press, 1977.

———. *Philosophy of Mind*. Oxford: Clarendon, 1971.

Helm, Paul. *John Calvin's Ideas*. Oxford: Oxford University Press, 2004.

Hitchens, Christopher. *God is Not Great: How Religion Poisons Everything*. New York: Hachette, 2007.

Hinde, Robert A. *Why Gods Persist: A Scientific Approach to Religion*. London: Routledge, 1999.

Hobbes, Thomas. *Leviathan*. Baltimore: Penguin Books, 1968.

Hume, David. *Dialogues Concerning Natural Religion* (1779). Indianapolis: Hackett Publishing Company, 1980.

———. *A Treatise of Human Nature*. Edited by L. A. Selby-Bigge. Oxford: Clarendon Press, 1555 (1888).

James, William. *Varieties of Religious Experience: A Study in Human Nature*. New York: Longmans, Green, 1902.

———. *The Will to Believe and Other Essays*. New York: Longsman, Green, 1912.

Janowski, Zbigniew. *Cartesian Theodicy: Descartes' Quest for Certitude*. Dordrecht: Kluwer, 2000.

Jones, David Albert. *Angels: A History*. Oxford: Oxford University Press, 2010.

Kant, Immanuel. *Critique of Pure Reason*. London: Macmillan, 1909.

Kierkegaard, Søren. *Christian Discourses*. Princeton: Princeton University Press, 1974.

———. *Sickness Unto Death*. Princeton: Princeton University Press, 1980.

———. *Practice in Christianity*. Princeton: Princeton University Press, 1991.

Klein, Kenneth H. *Positivism and Christianity: A Study of Theism and Verifiability*. The Hague: Martinus Nijhoff, 1974.

Kolakowski, Leszek. *God Owes Us Nothing: A Brief Remark on Pascal's Religion and on the Spirit of Jansenism*. Chicago: University of Chicago Press, 1995.

———. *Religion If There Is No God: On God, the Devil, Sin, and Other Worries of the So-Called Philosophy of Religion*. South Bend: St. Augustine's Press, 2001.

Kurz, Paul, ed. *Science and Religion: Are They Compatible*. Amherst: Prometheus Books, 2003.

La Haye, Tim & Jerry B. Jenkins. *Left Behind*. Wheaton: Tyndale, 1995.

————. *Glorious Appearing*. Wheaton: Tyndale House, 2004.

Laporte, Jean. *Le Coeur et la raison selon Pascal*. Paris: Éditions Elzévir, 1903.

Lennon, Thomas M. "Theology and the God of the Philosophers," in Donald Rutherford (ed.) *The Cambridge Companion to Early Modern Philosophy*, Cambridge: Cambridge University Press, 2006, pp. 274–298.

Libet, Benjamin. *Mind Time: The Temporal Factor in Consciousness*. Cambridge: Harvard University Press, 2005.

Locke, John. *An Essay Concerning Human Understanding*. 2 Vols. New York: Dover, 1959.

Loyola, Ignatius. *Letters and Instructions*. St. Louis: Institute of Jesuit Sources, 2006.

Ludwin, D. M. *Blaise Pascal's Quest for the Ineffable*. New York: Peter Lang, 2001.

Lycan, William G. & Jesse Prinz, eds. *Mind and Cognition*. Oxford: Basil Blackwell, 1999.

Maia Neto, Jose Raimundo. *The Christianization of Pyrrhonism: Scepticism and Faith in Pascal, Kierkegaard, and Shestov*. Dordrecht: Kluwer Academic Publishers, 1995.

Malebranche, Nicolas. *The Search After Truth*. Tr. by Thomas M. Lennon and Paul J. Olscamp. Columbus: Ohio State University Press, 1980.

Marion, Jean-Luc. *God Without Being*. Chicago: University of Chicago Press, 1991.

Matson, Wallace I. *The Existence of God*. Ithaca: Cornell University Press, 1965.

McGinn, Colin. *The Mysterious Flame: Conscious Minds in a Material World*. New York: Basic Books, 1999.

Menn, Stephen. *Descartes and Augustine*. Cambridge: Cambridge University Press, 1998.

Miel, Jan. *Pascal and Theology*. Baltimore: Johns Hopkins Press, 1969.

Nadler, Steven M. "Scientific Certainty and the Creation of the Eternal Truths: A Problem in Descartes," *Southern Journal of Philosophy*, Vol. 25, 1987, pp. 175–192.

———. *Spinoza's Heresy: Immortality and the Jewish Mind*. Oxford: Clarendon, 2001.

———. *A Book Forged in Hell: Spinoza's Scandalous Treatise and the Birth of the Secular Age*. Princeton: Princeton University Press, 2011.

Newberg, Andrew and Mark Robert Waldman. *How God Changes Your Brain*. New York: Ballantine Books, 2009.

Nye, Andrea. *The Princess and the Philosopher: Elisabeth of the Palatine to René Descartes*. Lanham: Rowan & Littlefield, 1999.

Ockham, William. *Predestination, God's Foreknowledge, and Future Contingents*. New York: Appleton-Century-Crofts, 1969.

O'Connell, Marvin R. *Blaise Pascal: Reasons of the Heart*. Grand Rapids: William B. Eerdmanns, 1997.

O'Donnell, James J. *Augustine: A New Biography*. New York: Harper, Collins, 2005.

Onfray, Michel. *Atheist Manifesto: The Case Against Christianity, Judaism, and Islam*. New York: Arcade Publishing, 2007.

Pagels, Elaine. *The Gnostic Gospels*. New York: Vintage Books, 1979.

———. *Adam, Eve, and the Serpent*. New York: Random House, 1988.

———. *Beyond Belief: The Secret Gospel of Thomas*. New York: Random House, 2003.

———. *Revelations*. New York: Viking, 2012.

Pagels, Elaine and Karen L. King. *Reading Judas: The Gospel of Judas and the Shaping of Christianity*. London: Penguin Books, 2008.

Palm, Franklin Charles. *Calvinism and the Religious Wars.* New York: Henry Holt, 1932.

Pascal, Blaise. *Oeuvres complètes.* Ed. Louis Lafuma. Paris: Éditions du Seuil, 1963.

———. *Pensées.* Translated by A. J. Krailsheimer. London: Penguin, revised 1995.

Paley, William. *Natural Theology, or Evidences of the Existence and the Attributes of the Deity.* Oxford: Oxford University Press, 2006.

Parsons, Keith. *God and the Burden of Proof: Plantinga, Swinburne, and the Analytical Defense of Theism.* Amherst: Prometheus Books, 1989.

Pelagius. *The Letters of Pelagius.* Everham: Arthur James, 1995.

Pepperberg, I. Maxine. *The Alex Studies: Cognitive and Communicative Abilities of Grey Parrots.* Cambridge: Harvard University Press, 2002.

———. *Alex and Me.* New York: Collins, 2008.

Pinker, Steven. *The Blank Slate: The Modern Denial of Human Nature.* New York: Viking, 2002.

Plantinga, Alvin. *God and Other Minds: A Study of the Rational Justification of Belief in God.* Ithaca: Cornell University Press, 1967.

———. "Reason and Belief in God," in Alvin Plantinga & Nicholas Wolterstorff, editors, *Faith and Rationality: Reason and Belief in God.* Notre Dame: University of Notre Dame Press, 1983.

———. *Where the Conflict Really Lies: Science, Religion, and Naturalism.* New York: Oxford University Press, 2012.

Plato. *Collected Dialogues.* New York: Bollingen Foundation, 1961.

Popkin, Richard H. *The History of Scepticism from Savonarola to Bayle.* Oxford: Oxford University Press, 2003.

———. *Spinoza.* Oxford: Oneworld, 2004.

Popkin, Richard H. & Arjo Vanderjagt, eds. *Scepticism and Irreligion in the Seventeenth and Eighteenth Centuries.* Leiden: E. J. Brill, 1993.

Roberts, James D. *Faith and Reason: A Comparative Study of Pascal, Bergson, and James*. Boston: Christopher Publishing House, 1962.

Royce, Josiah. *The Religious Aspect of Philosophy*. Boston: Houghton Mifflin, 1855.

———. *The Conception of God*. New York: Macmillan, 1897.

Russell, Paul. *The Riddle of Hume's Treatise: Skepticism, Naturalism, and Irreligion*. Oxford: Oxford University Press, 2008.

Rynin, David. "Cognitive Meaning and Cognitive Use." *Inquiry*, Vol. 9, 1996, pp. 109–131.

Rynin, David. "Vindication of L*G*C*L*P*S*T*V*S*M." *Proceedings and Addresses of the American Philosophical Association*, Vol. 30, 1957, pp. 45–67.

Schmidt, Albert-Marie. *Calvin and the Calvinistic Tradition*. New York: Harper & Brothers, 1960.

Schopenhauer, Arthur. *The World as Will and Idea*. London: Kegan Paul, Trench, Trubner, 1915.

Searle, John. *Minds, Brains, and Science*. Cambridge: Harvard University Press, 1984.

———. *The Rediscovery of the Mind*. Cambridge: MIT Press, 1992.

———. *The Mystery of Consciousness*. New York: New York Review, 1997.

Stegner, Victor J. *God: The Failed Hypothesis: How Science Shows That God Does Not Exist*. Amherst: Prometheus Books, 2007.

Steiner, Gary. *Descartes As A Moral Thinker: Christianity, Technology, Nihilism*. Amherst: Humanity Books, 2004.

Stillingfleet, Edward. *A Discourse in Vindication of the Doctrine of the Trinity: With an Answer to the Late Socinian Objections against it from Scripture, Antiquity, and Reason*. London: 1696.

Toland, John. *Christianity Not Mysterious: or, A Treatise Showing, That there is nothing in the GOSPEL Contrary to REASON, nor ABOVE it: And that no Christian Doctrine can be properly call'd a MYSTERY*. London: 1696.

Voltaire, François-Marie Arouet. *Candide and Other Writings*. New York: Modern Library, 1956.

Watson, Richard A. *Cogito Ergo Sum: The Life of René Descartes*. Boston: David R. Godine, second revised edition, 2007.

———. "Descartes Knows Nothing," in *The Breakdown of Cartesian Metaphysics*. Indianapolis: Hackett, 1998, pp. 193–203.

———. *The Philosopher's Diet: How to Lose Weight and Change the World*. Boston: David R. Godine, 1998.

———. *Descartes's Ballet: His Doctrine of the Will and His Political Philosophy*. South Bend: St. Augustine's Press, 2007.

Webb, Clement C. J. *Pascal's Philosophy of Religion*. Oxford: Clarendon Press, 1929.

Wetsel, David. *Pascal and Disbelief: Catechesis and Conversion in the Pensées*. Washington, D.C.: Catholic University of America Press, 1994.

Wills, Garry. *Saint Augustine*. New York: Viking, 1999.

Wolterstorff, Nicholas. "Can Belief in God be Rational If It Has No Foundations?" in Alvin Plantinga & Nicholas Wolterstorff, editors, *Faith and Rationality: Reason and Belief in God*, Notre Dame: University of Notre Dame Press, 1983.

———. "Introduction" in Alvin Plantinga & Nicholas Wolterstorff, editors, *Faith and Rationality: Reason and Belief in God*, Notre Dame: University of Notre Dame Press, 1983.

Zagajewski, Adam. *Canvas: Poems*. New York: Farrar Straus Giroux, 1971, p. 71, "From the Lives of Things."

Index